A GUIDE TO
DECORATION
IN THE
EARLY AMERICAN MANNER

FRONTISPIECE: Small oblong tray with gold leaf and transparent painting, copied by Nadine Wilson from original owned by Mrs. Carl Neruer.

A GUIDE TO
DECORATION
IN THE
EARLY AMERICAN MANNER

by Nadine Cox Wilson

CHARLES E. TUTTLE COMPANY
Rutland, Vermont & Tokyo, Japan

Representatives

For Continental Europe:
BOXERBOOKS, INC., Zurich

For the British Isles:
PRENTICE-HALL INTERNATIONAL, INC., London

For Australasia:
PAUL FLESCH & CO., PTY. LTD., Melbourne

Published by the Charles E. Tuttle Company, Inc.
of Rutland, Vermont and Tokyo, Japan
with editorial offices at Suido 1-chome, 2-6.
Bunkyo-ku, Tokyo, Japan

Book design and typography by
Keiko Chiba

Printed in Japan

Dedicated to

The students in my classes in
Early American Decoration at
The Riverside Church, New York

Table of Contents

List of Illustrations   11
Acknowledgments   13
Preliminary Remarks   15
Authentic Types of Trays   17
Complete List of Materials   22
Backgrounds   30
First Process: Tracing a Stencil Pattern   42
Second Process: Cutting the Stencil   46
Third Process: Application of the Stencil   50
Fourth Process: Striping   59
Fifth Process: Tinting the Stencil   63
Sixth Process: Freehand Brush Strokes   67
Seventh Process: Country Painting   78
Eighth Process: Freehand Bronze   82
Ninth Process: Gold Leaf   86
Tenth Process: Floating Color   93
Eleventh Process: Lace-Edge Painting   98
Bibliography   103
Addresses for Materials   107
Index   111

List of Illustrations

Frontispiece. Small oblong tray with gold leaf and transparent
       painting
1, 2.   Authentic types of trays in various shapes
       and designs 18, 20
3–5.   Brushes and brush boxes 23–24
6.   Sableline varnish brush and container 25
7.   All-purpose decorating kit 26
8.   Folding card table adapted for work table 26
9.   Copying an original design 44–45
10.   Cutting a stencil 47
11.   Composite stencil 47
12.   One-piece stencil 48
13.   Composite design copied from Hitchcock chair 49
14.   Composite design of many units 49
15.   One-piece stencil copied from document box 49
16.   Preparation of velour palette 51
17.   Modeled leaves with veining shaded by S curve 54
18.   Leaves with veins cut out in linen 55
19, 20.   Methods of veining leaves; silhouette leaves 55
21.   Stenciling with a composite stencil and a one-
      piece unit 57
22.   Striping the flange of a tray 60
23.   Care of the paint brush 64
24.   Brush strokes in fine-tailed style 71
25.   Brush strokes in knife-edge style 72–73

26. Brush strokes in teardrop style 72–73
27. Basic brush strokes 74
28. Freehand brush strokes 75
29. Use of the sable scroller 76
30. Scroll made with sable scroller 77
31. Transferring the design to the article 81
32. Painting a freehand bronze design 83
33. Design painted in freehand bronze 83
34. Laying gold leaf on tin or wood 90
35. Tray with applied gold leaf 91
36. Preparation for tracing a design 96

12

Acknowledgments

In the writing of this book I am indebted to the following people: First of all to my son, Robert Dean Wilson, for taking the photographs for the illustrations. I have received invaluable aid in editing and typing from Mrs. Margaret Stoffregen. I am also indebted to my husband, Dr. Harry R. Wilson, for his understanding and patience while I was working on the book and to Emily Rich Underhill for the suggestions she made after reading the manuscript.

Preliminary Remarks

The art of early American decoration refers to the manner in which the early settlers of this country decorated the walls, floors, furniture, tinware, and many wooden objects used in their homes.

This guide is an attempt to present materials and procedures which will help you to master the different techniques which were used. Practically all of the techniques were brought over by the early Americans as they migrated from their native countries. Later, as the machine age developed in our country, these techniques were gradually replaced by other methods. As these early techniques became neglected, understanding and knowledge about them almost disappeared. Through years of research and experimentation, Esther Stevens Brazer and others have revived these techniques. Because of their efforts, we are now able to reproduce many beautiful designs in the original authentic manner. Each period and country produced its own style and technique. For this reason, if you want to reproduce work in the authentic style of a particular period or country, you must reproduce each design by executing it in the appropriate technique.

It becomes a most fascinating game and pastime to search for the old tray, tin box, chair, chest, or article on which you wish to reproduce a design. Occasionally, while searching for an antique article to decorate, you may come across one with the design so well preserved that you may wish to keep it in its

15

original state. (How to preserve a design is described on p. 32–33.) If an original article is not available, several companies are now making beautiful reproductions of old tinware which are quite satisfactory for this work.

If you are looking for an artistic recreation, you will find the techniques which were used in early American decoration most interesting. Moreover, the practical use to which you can put the results of your own efforts is most gratifying. Your home can be made more attractive, and your art work will give it more individuality. Your friends will cherish the gifts which you make for them.

Also, with the increased interest in early American decoration, what may be described as a pleasurable avocation may even become a profitable vocation. The Esther Stevens Brazer Guild of the Historical Society of Early American Decoration, founded in honor of Esther Stevens Brazer, points out the fact that throughout the country there are calls for teachers of this early American art. Department stores are asking almost prohibitive prices for furniture and tinware decorated in the early American manner. Of course, to attain the perfection necessary for professional work, you must be willing to give continuous time and energy as well as assiduous study to the acquisition of the variety of techniques and the knowledge of history which this exacting art demands.

Many novices become discouraged and disillusioned in attempting to master the variety of techniques necessary to do authentic work. Artistic results do require patience and time. However, if a step-by-step approach is taken, you will gain control of the various processes presented in this booklet. Progress will be realized immediately. You will gradually experience the pleasure of creating something of your own in this fascinating art work.

Authentic Types of Trays

Of all the various aspects of early American decoration, the stenciling and japanning of tin trays continues to be the most popular. Japanning is the art of producing highly varnished surfaces, like those of oriental lacquer work, on wood, metal, or papier-mâché, plain or ornamented. Early tin was made by the difficult task of coating iron plates with a thin layer of tin. By 1720 the making of tin plate was well established in England. Edward Allgood discovered a method of japanning tin plate in Pontypool, Wales, but he died in 1763 before the process was developed.

The work was carried on for many years by his son Thomas. In 1763 another branch of the family established a second manufactory of japan ware at Usk, Wales. From these two sources the finest examples of japan ware were exported all over the world. Since this booklet is devoted primarily to the techniques used in decorating various types of trays, it seems necessary to give some approximate dates and descriptions of the trays characteristic of the various periods. Many original shapes of japan ware are being reproduced in this country today.

1. Lace-edge trays, so called because of the pierced lace-like edge, were round, oval, or rectangular. Sometimes they were equipped with ornamental brass handles. Some were not pierced but still were painted in the same style. A characteristic of the design found on these trays was the extreme highlights blending with very dark transparent colors which faded off

PLATE 1. Authentic types of trays: (upper left) oval lace-edge with original design; (upper right) oval gallery with keyhole flange; (lower left) deep-edge octagonal; (lower right) rectangular with original design in floating color and gold-leaf border.

into the background. The design generally consisted of roses or other flowers, fruits, a bird, or an urn draped with a swag. Surrounding the center motif were scattered sprays of flowers. The background was often painted in a tortoise-shell effect with a fine gold-leaf border close to the pierced rim. Paul Revere began importing these trays from England to Boston in 1785.

18

Although others imported these trays, they are still often called Revere trays.

2. Gallery trays were oval and closely related to the lace-edge trays in decoration, although some had fine painted landscapes. The edge was perpendicular, with a keyhole piercing, although there were some with a plain edge. There were also gallery trays with elaborate gold-leaf border designs and fine pen work. These trays were made from about 1780 on through the Sheraton and Hepplewhite periods.

3. Deep-edged octagonal trays date approximately from 1765 to 1820, until the stenciled rectangular trays came into existence. These trays were sometimes decorated with classical gold-leaf double borders. Later ones occasionally had stenciled borders with many freehand details painted in. Some had a landscape medallion in the center, painted in natural colors.

4. Rectangular trays date approximately from 1760 to 1918. The earlier types often had a flat narrow flange or rim. The designs were of very intricate gold leaf and fine pen work. Some borders were painted in freehand gold leaf, and the centers consisted of flowers or birds painted with the floating color technique. Floating is the process of flowing transparent color overtones on top of an underlying pattern so that all sharp lines are softened into subtle shading which melts away into nothingness. The later trays had wider flanges of two and a half to three inches. A greater variety of designs appeared on these trays.

5. Chippendale, Gothic, or pie crust trays date approximately from 1750 to 1870. The earlier trays had freehand gold-leaf painting of very fine and detailed design, including scrolls of gold leaf and fine pen work. Sometimes flowers of subdued colors were intermingled with the gold-leaf border and dripping vines. About the year 1800 a type of Gothic tray called Gothic Sandwich was made with a perfectly flat outer section on the edge. Many of the Gothic Sandwich trays were ornamented with floral sprays at the edge only. From 1838 on, during the Victorian period, designs of fountains and beautiful birds with iridescent colored breasts which were painted over an under-

19

PLATE 2. Authentic types of trays: (upper left) Chippendale with original gold-leaf design; (upper right) oblong stenciled, reproduced from an original; (lower left) cut-corner "coffin" tray with country painting, copied by Nadine Wilson from original owned by Margaret Watts; (lower right) Queen Anne.

lying layer of gold or silver leaf came into vogue. They were painted in floating color and were often enriched with mother-of-pearl and gold leaf. Similar trays were also made of papier-mâché and decorated in the same manner. Stencils were not used on these trays.

6. Oblong stenciled trays appeared in America in 1817. Un-

20

til about 1825 the composite design with the modeled leaf, made by shading over the curved edge of architect's linen, was used. Many shades of bronze powders were skillfully blended to give color and variety. Lates the veins for leaves were cut out of one piece of architect's linen, and landscapes and scenes began to appear. By 1845 stencils were cut in one piece, and a wash of transparent oil colors mixed with varnish was floated over the gold and silver patterns.

7. Country tin trays, often called octagonals or coffin lid trays, were made in this country by the Patterson Brothers who came from Ireland and settled in Berlin, Connecticut about 1738. Edward and William Patterson (sometimes spelled Pattison) established the first manufactory of tinware in the colonies sometime between 1740–1750. They imported from England tin plates which were made in two sizes, 11 7/8 × 9 inches and 18 3/8 × 11 inches. Making a tray larger than the size of the tin plate necessitated piecing two sheets of tin plate together and making a seam down the middle. Therefore, a seamed tray would predate any tray made after electroplating came into general use in about 1830. These octagonal trays had a very narrow, slanted flange. The backgrounds were usually painted black or asphaltum, but sometimes the backgrounds were painted Prussian blue, red, yellow, or white. They were decorated in gay primary colors with simple brush-stroke patterns. Sometimes the decoration throughout Maine, New Hampshire, Connecticut, New York, and Pennsylvania was done by the country tinsmith. Often a colorful design was superimposed on a wide white band which was painted next to the flange. Since most small shops could not afford the imported metal-leaf and bronze powders, they were seldom used on these trays.

8. Queen Anne trays, which appeared from the early 1700's to about 1750, were unique in their shape. They were influenced by the Queen Anne period of architecture of the early 18th century. The Queen Anne tray was often decorated in gold-leaf scroll work with a floral design in the center.

Complete List of Materials

Success in this work depends upon having the proper equipment and materials at hand at all times. Therefore, it is advisable for you to assemble a complete kit of materials as soon as possible. The following list includes everything you will need to master the techniques presented in this booklet. In several of the listings you will find a choice of brands of paints, varnishes, etc., all of which have proved satisfactory. Some of these products are difficult to obtain in certain localities. Besides this master list, a specific list of materials will be given at the beginning of each process presented.

Tools

Basket, small suitcase, or box for carrying tools and equipment
Fine stencil scissors, straight and curved edges
Scissors for cutting linen and paper
Single edge, steel-back razor blades (Gem) or Grifhold all-purpose knife #119 used with Christy surgical blades #11
Hawk Crow quill pen #107 and holder or Rapidograph Technical Fountain Pen #00 extra fine, which is expensive but well worth the money
Hunts bowl point pen #512
Pen #311, Brandeau & Company, for extra fine pen work
Etching needles which can be made by inserting a needle into a pen holder and gluing it with liquid solder
Hard Arkansas oil stone (pocket size) $3'' \times 1'' \times 1/4''$, HB-13s, Behr-Manning Co.

22

Grifhold Stencil Knife #3, 1/16″ blade
Rubber dam punch
Revolving leather punch #225
Palette knife
Pliers
Paint scraper
Soft Pink Pearl peel-off pencil eraser #400
Erasing shield
Gold and silver or white Eagle Turquoise pencil #938 or Stabilo #8052 which will write on anything
Piece of glass on which to cut stencils, about 8″ × 10″
Paint palette, peel-off type, or a piece of white tile
Charcoal stumps for freehand bronzing
Ordinary can opener
Old spoon
Paper clips
Small baby bottle, with nipple top cut off, in which to hang varnish brush
Magnifying glasses

Brushes

Art & Sign, French quill brushes, also called square shaders, series #474 or #475, sizes 0 through 8. Wooden handles to fit

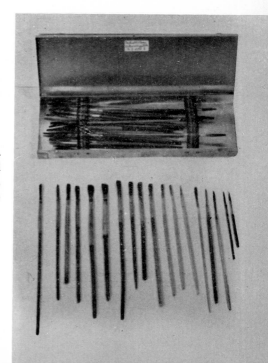

PLATE 3. Brushes: (above) aluminum box for holding short-handled brushes; (below) French quill, square-tipped, camel-hair brushes, with handles inserted.

PLATE 4. Brushes: (above) aluminum box for holding long-handled brushes; (below) pointed sable water-color brushes.

PLATE 5. Brushes: (above) aluminum box for holding long-handled brushes; (below) square-tipped sable brushes.

24

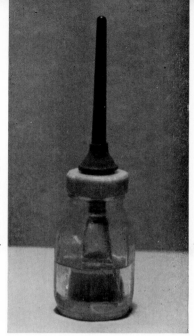

PLATE 6. Brushes: sableline varnish brush hung in baby's even-flow orange-juice bottle. The top is cut off the nipple, and a handle is inserted. The brush hairs must not touch the bottom of the bottle. The bottle is filled with just enough turpentine to cover the ferrule of the brush.

Art & Sign, series #914, 1/4″ and 3/4″

    or M. Grumbacher, series #6661, 1/4″ and 3/4″

M. Grumbacher, brights brushes, series #626-B, sizes 1 through 12

    or Art & Sign, brights brushes, series #823, sizes 1 through 12

Art & Sign, liners, also called scrollers, series #832, sizes 0 and 1 or series #831, sizes 1 and 2

    or M. Grumbacher, liners, series #7356, sizes 1 and 2

Art & Sign, The Spotter, size 00, 000, or 0000, for clean-up

Sword striping brush, size 00

Art & Sign, Sabeline brush, series #1825, 1″, hung in a bottle of turpentine, for varnishing

Sable or ox hair brushes, 2″ wide, one each for painting the primer coats and the background colors

Sable water color brushes, a selection from one of the following series:

    Art & Sign, Finepoint, series #9, sizes 0 through 8

    Art & Sign, Everpoint, series #8, sizes 0 through 8

    M. Grumbacher, series #197, sizes 1 through 8

    Winsor & Newton, Ltd., series #7, sizes 0 through 8

Soft camel's hair brush for brushing off gold leaf

25

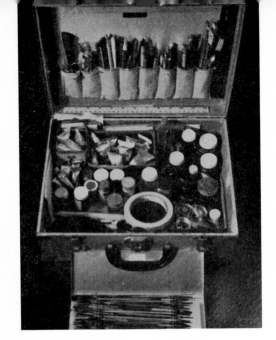

PLATE 7. All-purpose decorating kit.

PLATE 8. Folding card table adapted for work table. It can be set up in any convenient and available space.

26

Bronze Powders (lining powders)
Manufactured by Uhlfelder, Drakenfeld, or Baer Bros.
Smooth Butler's Silver
Rich gold
Pale gold
Antique gold
Orange Schliff
Venus extra brilliant fire bronze
Copper, finest
Statuary
Belvedere
Patent green
Paints and Varnishes
1. *Tube Paints* (*small tubes*)
   Japan colors (opaque colors)
     Sign craft red
     Venetian red
     Chrome yellow, medium
     Striping white
   Artist oil colors (Winsor-Newton or Grumbacher pre-tested)
     Prussian blue
     Alizarin crimson
     Indian yellow or yellow lake
     English vermilion, Devoe
   Raw umber
   Burnt umber
   Burnt sienna
   Yellow ochre
   Titanium white
2. *Flat Background Paints*
   Sta Blac Enamel 13, Pratt and Lambert
   Flat Black #152, Lowe Bros.
   Flat Black Waterspar Enamel, Pittsburgh
   Flat Black Enameloid, Sherwin-Williams
   Satin Impervo, Benjamin Moore & Co.
   Utilac Enamel, Benjamin Moore & Co.

27

3. *Primer Coats for Metal*
   Effecto Enamel White, Pratt and Lambert
   Primer Coat for Metal, Duco
   Red Sanding Primer, A & D
   P.C. #77 Clear, De Rusto
4. *Paint Removers*
   Wonder Paste, Wilson-Imperial
   TM-4, Winfield Brooks
   Strip-Ez
   Kwikleen Remover, Franklin & Lennon Paint Co.
5. *Rust Removers*
   Rust-i-cide
6. *Size for Laying Gold Leaf*
   Quick-Drying Gold Size, Nobles & Hoare
   Quick-Drying Gold Size, clear synthetic, Hastings
   Slow-Drying Mixtion Clarifée, Le Franc, Paris
   Slow-Drying Oil Gold Size, yellow, Hastings
   Slow-Drying Oil Gold Size, clear, Hastings

Varnishes

Floor Varnish, #61 Clear, Pratt and Lambert
Master-Mix Spar Varnish, Sears Roebuck
Black Seal, Giles
Plax, #826 Holland Yellow, Lowe Bros.
Asphaltum Varnish, Murphy

Miscellaneous Materials

Black Hazencote paper (Hazen Paper Co.), Black Croyden
   (Milton Paper Co.), or Dura-Glo (Henry Lindenmeyer & Son)
Architect's tracing linen (be careful never to get a drop of water
   on it)
Very fine tracing paper
Graphite paper
Frosted Protectoid, Frosted Cellophane, Supersee, or Traceolene,
   all of which will be referred to as frosted acetate. Medium
   weight, AB 301
Clear Cellophane #300, which will be referred to as acetate

28

Roll of ordinary wax paper
Chair-Loc
Roll of masking tape
Fine sandpaper
Fine wet or dry sandpaper #600
Steel wool #0000
Artone India Ink, Fine Line, black
Small bottle of household ammonia
Small bottle of turpentine
Carbon tetrachloride, Carbona, Renuzit, Wilson's Imperial Brush Cleaner, or Kem
Square cake of carbonate of magnesium (obtain at drugstore) or Lithopone
Dental pumice powder (obtain at drugstore)
Rotten stone (obtain at paint store)
Crude oil (obtain at paint store)
Bottle of clear nail polish
Blackboard eraser for rubbing the final finish
Old nylon stockings, cut in 3 or 4 pieces, used for applying varnish on paper
Sponge cloth (obtain at hardware store)
Tack cloth
Lard oil, Neatsfoot Oil, or Stat
Old cotton rags, lint-free
Cake of Lava soap, Proctor & Gamble
Le Page's liquid solder (small tube)
Piece of cotton-backed velour, about 12″×14″, hemmed or bound, used for bronze powder palette
Squares of silk-backed velvet, about 4 1/2″, used as a finger for applying bronze powders
Small velvet bobs: Make various sizes with small pieces of velvet wrapped around the end of a Q-Tip and fastened with an elastic band
Piece of *new* fur, such as nutria, sable, beaver, or mink
Book of gold leaf, palladium leaf, or silver leaf
Master Medium, Bohemian Wax

Patina or any good paste wax, for tole or wood
Old tooth brush
Cord or twine
Newspapers
Tin cans for mixing paints
Cardboard
Wrapping paper
Tin lids
Table lamp with strong light for close work
Small medicine bottles with screw tops (make a collection)
Small bottle caps (remove rubber and cork)

Backgrounds

Before starting to master the different techniques outlined in the following processes, it is important to understand the preparation of the backgrounds before applying the decoration on the tin or wood. Final decision on the selection of the background will depend upon the type of article and the design chosen for the article.

Materials Needed

Paint remover. The following three may be flushed off with water:
1. Wilson–Imperial Wonder Paste
2. TM–4
3. Kwikleen Remover

Old paint brush
Paint scraper
Old toothbrush
Cord or twine
Steel wool
Fine sandpaper
Newspapers
Old rags
Wet or dry sandpaper #600
Brush cleaner
Can for mixing paints
Rust-i-cide

Duratite wood filler
Metal primer
Shellac (for wood only)
Flat paint, black or color
Japan Venetian red
Paint brush
Can opener and old spoon
Varnish brush hung in turpentine
Alcohol
Hunts bowl point pen #512
Paste wax or Patina

Varnish   Rubbing oil or crude oil
Turpentine   Dental pumice
Asphaltum   Rotten stone
                            Blackboard eraser

Preparation of Various Backgrounds

An Original Design—How to Preserve

1. Make a solution of mild soap with a little ammonia and water. Wash the article with a soft sponge cloth. Rinse it well and dry it. Protect the surface with a coat of clear varnish.

2. If the first solution does not clean satisfactorily, a stronger solution can be used with great caution.

Solution: 1/3 Isopropyl alcohol
            1/3 Diacetone alcohol
            1/3 Acetone

3. Lightly dampen a soft cloth and wipe over a very small area at a time. Work fast to prevent the solution from softening the painted surface. When the entire surface is cleaned, wash, rinse, and dry the article. Protect it with a coat of clear varnish.

4. Rust spots on tin articles should be treated with Rust-i-cide, then painted over with background paint before the varnish is applied. Moisten a Q-Tip or piece of cotton rolled on a toothpick with Rust-i-cide. Apply this to spots, using care not to get Rust-i-cide on the painted surface. When the rust is dissolved, clean off the loose rust with a small piece of #0000 steel wool or #600 wet or dry sandpaper. Wash the entire article, rinse it well, and dry it. Paint the rust spots with the same color used on the background. If deep holes are left from the rust erosion, they can be filled in gradually. Mix a little dental pumice with the paint and fill the holes, allowing each filling to dry before adding another mixture. Continue this until the holes are even with the surface. Dry twenty-four hours. Sand the paint and dental pumice lightly. Protect the entire surface with a coat of clear varnish.

5. If the article is a rare, valuable piece, it would be advisable to build up a protection of many coats of varnish. Do not rub the surface smooth until three coats of varnish have been applied. Allow twenty-four hours between each coat. After the third coat has been applied, rub each succeeding coat smooth after the varnish has had twenty-four hours to dry. Use #600 wet or dry sandpaper and keep it wet. Lava soap or dental pumice may be added. When the final surface is smooth, make a paste of rotten stone and rubbing oil and rub the article with a felt blackboard eraser. Wash it thoroughly with a detergent. Apply any good paste wax. After the wax has dried, polish the article with a soft cloth. If this procedure is followed, the design will be protected for many years as a decorative piece. It will also hold up under normal use.

Old Tin—How to Strip

1. If the article has an original stencil worth copying, follow the instructions in "First Process," #6, p. 43, before stripping. If the original design is gold leaf, painted, or a combination of techniques, do not use architect's linen. Instead, after the ink drawing has been perfected on the tracing paper, place a piece of frosted acetate over the drawing and paint directly on the acetate.

2. Flow on the paint remover with an old brush and allow time for the paint to loosen.

3. Wipe off the loose paint with wadded newspaper. Be careful not to get any on your hands or clothing. Scrape stubborn spots with a paint scraper. Repeat this process until all the paint is soft. Clean the remaining spots with steel wool, then with wet or dry sandpaper. Flush off with water.

This process may be shortened if it is possible to make a lye bath which will cover the article. The article to be stripped can be left in the solution over night. Extreme caution must be taken not to splatter on anything or leave the solution where children can reach it.

4. Treat any rust spots with Rust-i-cide according to the intructions on the bottle.

33

5. Sand, wash with detergent and water, rinse well, and dry thoroughly. The tin is now ready for the first metal primer coat. All metal should be protected with two or three thin coats of metal primer. This prevents the tin from rusting and leaves a good base on which to paint.

New Tin

1. New tin is oiled by the manufacturer in order to preserve it. This oil should be wiped off with turpentine or alcohol before applying a metal primer coat.

Primer Coat for Tin

1. Mix the metal primer with turpentine to a thin consistency. Apply two or three coats twenty-four hours apart. Sand and wash each coat before applying the next coat. No brush strokes should remain. If De Rusto Primer is used, do not thin it with turpentine.

Old Wood—How to Strip

1. Follow the instructions for Old Tin #1, #2, and #3 above. Exception: Do not flush off the paint remover with water. Instead, wipe it off with a damp cloth or alcohol. An old toothbrush can be used to clean out grooves. Heavy cord or twine is useful for cleaning deep ridges on the rungs of chairs.

2. Fill any holes with Duratite and make any necessary repairs. Apply Chair-Loc, a liquid applied with a dropper, to any loose joints to tighten them.

3. Allow the Duratite to dry and sand the wood with medium-coarse sandpaper. Wipe clean and sand very smooth with fine sandpaper. Wipe clean.

4. Apply a thin coat of shellac. When it has dried, sand again and wipe clean. The surface is now ready for the first coat of paint.

New Wood

1. Sand smooth. Wipe clean and apply a coat of thinned shellac. Dry.

2. Sand with wet or dry sandpaper #600. Wipe clean and apply the background paint according to following instructions.

34

Painting the Background

Solid Opaque Background

Most decoration is more effective when painted on a black background. However, a dark green or red background, and even light colors, are sometimes used, but the black gives a greater contrast.

1. In a can, mix flat black or the color to be used to a thin consistency. Add a tablespoon of varnish and stir.

2. With long strokes, paint the prepared surface, leaving no brush strokes or drips.

3. Let the paint dry for twenty-four hours. Sand the surface lightly and then wipe it clean.

4. Repeat this process three or four times twenty-four hours apart, until a good smooth surface is obtained. When painting trays, turn the tray over and paint the back, alternating between back and front. Be sure to sand lightly between each coat and wipe clean. The surface is now ready to be varnished.

Transparent Background with Asphaltum Varnish

Usually the background of all old country tin is painted with a mixture of asphaltum varnish.

1. Mix varnish and a little asphaltum and then paint over the crystalized or shiny new tin. The color can be varied by adding a little alizarin crimson or yellow lake.

2. Bake it in an oven at 350°F for one hour.

3. Protect the surface with three coats of clear varnish before rubbing.

Tortoise-shell Background

This unusual background is most often found on much of the old lace-edge type of decoration.

Method One:

1. Paint patches of vermilion on a prepared black background. Let this dry for twenty-four hours.

2. Paint over the patches with a mixture of 1/3 varnish and 2/3 asphaltum.

35

3. While it is still wet, wipe out some of the mixture from the patches with a lint-free piece of sheet or linen.

Method Two:

1. Paint patches in an oyster shape with varnish or gold size.

2. Lay on palladium leaf, aluminum leaf, or silver leaf when the paint has reached the proper stickiness. Test with the tip of a finger or a piece of architect's linen. When this does not leave an imprint but still adheres slightly, it is of the proper stickiness. Dry.

3. Paint over the metal leaf with a mixture of alizarin crimson and burnt umber. Dry.

4. Paint over the metal patches with a mixture of 1/3 varnish and 2/3 asphaltum.

5. Remove some of the mixture over the patches while it is still wet, using a sheet or old linen, according to the effect desired.

Bronze or Dusted Background

This background is found mostly on Chippendale trays made of paper or tin and occasionally on rectangular trays and other articles.

1. Build up a smooth coat of black background.

2. Add a coat of clear varnish and allow the surface to become almost dry.

3. Start polishing the center with a pale gold bronze powder and work out to the edge, graduating the powders from deeper shades of gold to copper and blending the brown tone at the edges until it fades into nothingness. Always start back at the center and work out to the edge gradually. A piece of sable or mink fur will give a very smooth and blended background.

4. It may be necessary to repeat this process several times before the desired effect is reached. Be sure to wash off the excess powders each time before revarnishing.

5. When finished, protect the surface with a coat of varnish before decorating.

Artificial Graining on a Wood Background

Since most graining is done on soft wood such as pine, an

36

attempt was made to simulate the grain of the finer woods such as rosewood.

1. Prepare according to instructions for Old Wood above.
2. Mix japan Venetian red with turpentine to a thin consistency.
3. Paint the entire surface, leaving no brush strokes or drips.
4. Dry thoroughly—at least a week. Sand lightly and wipe clean.
5. Mix flat black with turpentine to a thin consistency.
6. With a one-inch oxhair brush, paint a strip to be grained. Quickly dip the brush into the thin black mixture and brush along the wet strip in a waving motion, imitating the natural graining in rosewood. Continue until the entire chair or area is grained.

There are other techniques of graining in addition to #6 above. The first step after painting the area with the thin black mixture is:

   a. Wiping off the black mixture while it is still damp with crumpled newspaper.
   b. Cutting irregular-size teeth on the edge of a piece of cardboard and dragging it along the damp black mixture.
   c. Lining up evenly a set of various size brushes and wiring them together. (The same effect can be obtained by cutting out hairs at irregular intervals from an old stiff brush). Dip them into the thin black mixture and brush according to the grain in the wood.
   d. Removing the paint with a stiff quill feather.

Each technique requires experimentation and practice. The slat on a chair to be stenciled or painted is usually left solid black.

Antiquing on a Decorated Background

Decorated articles can be made to look old by the process of antiquing. However, keep in mind that stenciling will antique itself in a short time. Bronze powders are made of brass, copper, silver, and other metals which tarnish even when protected with several coats of varnish. Any article should have one coat of varnish over the decoration before the antiquing is applied. Let dry for twenty-four hours.

1. Take a small amount of burnt umber, raw umber, or burnt sienna and dissolve it in a can with a little turpentine. Add varnish. Lamp black or yellow lake can be used instead of the umbers, depending on the desired effect.

2. Varnish over the first coat. A second coat of antiquing can be added the next day, if necessary.

3. Protect the antiquing with clear varnish, as directed under Final Varnish Finish, p. 40.

Varnishing the Background

Varnish Preliminary to Decoration

1. Select a dry day when the humidity is not over 70%.

2. Varnish in a room which is as dust-free as possible.

3. The varnish and the article to be varnished should be at room temperature.

4. Open a glossy magazine to a dust-free page and place it on the work table.

5. With a spoon, dip out of the can the amount of varnish to be used and put it in a clean container. Replace the lid on the varnish can and close it tightly.

Caution: Air causes varnish to become gummy and thick. If this happens, throw it away. It cannot be thinned. Never shake or stir varnish.

6. Wipe the surface to be varnished with a tack cloth or a sponge cloth dampened in a mixture of turpentine and water.

7. Wipe any turpentine out of the varnish brush with paper toweling or a lint-free rag.

8. Dip the brush into the varnish and press it on the sides of the can in order to eliminate excess varnish.

9. Take long quick strokes, and then crosshatch. Complete one area before moving on to the next. Start varnishing a tray on

the flange and pick up varnish as it runs down the sides. Continue until the floor of the tray is covered. The entire surface should be completed before the varnish has a chance to "set."

10. With the tip of the brush, "tip off" bubbles and lift any hairs or dust particles which may have fallen into the varnish. Stroke these out of the brush on a glossy magazine. Hold the tray up to the light and tilt it to make sure every spot has been covered. Run the moist brush around the edge of the flange and the hand holes to pick up any drips.

11. Place the article in a level position in a dust-free closet, drawer, or box.

12. Let it dry for at least twenty-four hours.

13. Reverse the tray and varnish the back at least twice, twenty-four hours apart.

14. Rub the top of the tray with wet or dry sandpaper #600. Keep it wet. Wash and dry.

15. Apply a second coat of varnish in the same manner as the first.

16. Let it dry at least twenty-four hours.

17. Rub it again with wet or dry sandpaper #600. Add a little Lava soap and keep the tray wet. If all the bubbles and dust spots are rubbed to a smooth dull finish, the article is ready to decorate.

18. In some instances, it is necessary to stripe before decorating. If this is the case, striping may be done after the second coat of varnish has been rubbed smooth and dull.

19. In twenty-four hours protect the striping with another coat of varnish before proceeding with the decoration.

Final Varnish Finish

When all the decorating has been completed, make a mixture of varnish and gold powder in a bottle cap. Dip a Hunts bowl point pen #512 into this mixture and sign your name and date on the back of the article. Make sure the decoration is thoroughly dry before applying the first coat of varnish. Gold leaf and lace edge take much longer to dry than paint mixed with varnish.

39

1. Varnish in the same way as described above in Varnish Preliminary to Decoration. Do not rub the first coat because you may rub through to the design.

2. The second varnish coat should be rubbed lightly. Be careful not to rub through.

3. After the third coat of varnish has dried, rub with wet or dry sandpaper #600, dental pumice, and water until all the bumps disappear. Several more coats of varnish may be necessary in order to obtain a perfectly smooth surface. Rub the surface smooth between each coat.

4. In order to make the article alcohol-proof, the last coat should be varnished with a hard water-proof and alcohol-proof varnish. Rub the final coat of varnish smooth with dental pumice, water, and wet or dry sandpaper #600. Wash and dry.

5. Make a paste of rubbing oil or crude oil and rotten stone. Dip a felt blackboard eraser into the mixture and rub. Keep the eraser moist with oil and rotten stone. The longer you rub, the finer the surface becomes.

6. Wash the article thoroughly with detergent and water. Rinse well and dry.

7. Wax with any good paste wax. Dry. Polish. Or apply Patina, which also gives a nice luster, instead of wax, according to directions on the can.

How to Make a Tack Cloth

Dampen an old piece of fine handkerchief linen and wring it dry. Dampen it with turpentine and add two tablespoons of varnish. Squeeze the linen and rub the mixture in well. Put the cloth in a closed glass jar. Add a little water and turpentine as it dries out.

How to Make a Burnt Varnish Ball

Put rosin in a tin can which is set in a pan of water to avoid its *exploding* and heat slowly. Stir it with a wooden stick. Add

40

varnish as needed, making the mixture more or less one part rosin to six parts varnish. After the mixture has been prepared and allowed to cool, put it in a jar until it is needed. When it is necessary to pick up particles of dust, lift a small portion of this mixture out of the jar and roll it between the fingers into a soft ball. Fasten the ball on the end of a pen nib or pencil and lift off the particles.

Further Suggestions

Articles which do not need to be protected from water and alcohol can by varnished with a dull or low-luster varnish. Several are listed below:

Impervo Satin Finish, Benjamin Moore & Co.

Mar-Not Satin Finish, Sherwin-Williams

Duncan Phyfe, Valentine

Chippendale Varnish, Valentine

Super Valspar Low Luster, Valspar Corp.

Do not use the same brush which was used for a high-gloss varnish.

Never apply dull varnish until the article is first varnished with a high-gloss varnish.

Dull varnish does not need to be rubbed. It may be waxed; however, it will never attain the look of a hand-rubbed surface.

White or light backgrounds should be protected with a clear varnish such as McCloskey's Heirloom Crystal Clear Gloss Varnish.

FIRST PROCESS

Tracing a Stencil Pattern

Materials Needed

Architect's linen
Fine tracing paper
Frosted acetate
Scissors
Stencil scissors
Artone India ink, fine line
Crow quill pen, Hawk Point #107 or Rapidograph fountain pen
Small bottle of ammonia
Masking tape
Cotton rags
White pencil, Eagle #938 Turquoise or Stabilo #8052
Piece of cardboard for keeping the pieces of linen flat, enclosed in a wax paper envelope

Composite and One-Piece Stencils

Before copying a stencil, it is necessary to distinguish between a composite stencil and a one-piece stencil. The early stencils were composite stencils. They consisted of many units which were stenciled one behind the other, leaving a blended dark shadow. In the later stencils, which were cut out of one piece of linen, there was a definite space, often called a "bridge," surrounding each unit of the design. A slight distinction is also made in the procedure depending on whether the pattern is traced from a stencil pattern or from an original piece.

42

Procedure

1. Cut a piece of architect's linen large enough to fit the *stencil pattern*, leaving at least a one-inch margin all around. If the design is a composite one, cut a piece for each unit, leaving the inch margin, before you start to copy.

2. Place the linen, dull side up, over the stencil or unit and fasten it down at the corners with small pieces of masking tape.

3. With a crow quill pen and Artone ink, trace the design on the linen. Use a light stroke making as fine a line as possible. If the pen becomes clogged with ink, dip it in ammonia and clean it with a cloth.

4. Write your name, the date, and number of the pattern in the corner of each piece of linen.

5. Cut a piece of cardboard, slightly larger than the largest stencil pattern. Write your name, the date, and number of this pattern on the back of the cardboard; also number the pieces of linen. Lay the linen tracings flat on the cardboard. Place the cardboard on a piece of wax paper and fold the wax paper over the edges of the cardboard. If necessary, use a paper clip to hold it in place. This will keep the linen flat and in place until you are ready to cut the stencils.

6. If the pattern is traced from an *original piece* rather than a stencil pattern, the procedure is somewhat different. The article should be washed clean with soap and water. Sometimes a quick rub with Isopropyl alcohol or a thin coat of varnish brushed over the worn off parts will clarify the pattern. After this is done, hold the article in the sun or a strong light, and usually the extremely worn places can be faintly distinguished. Trace around the edges of these worn off places with a white pencil or white ink. Place fine frosted acetate dull side up over the entire pattern. Fasten the acetate with masking tape and trace the pattern with a crow quill pen and India ink. Remove the tracing, mount it on cardboard, and place ordinary tracing paper over the original tracing. Make the necessary corrections and perfect the drawing.

43

PLATE 9. How to copy an original design. *a.* Original design of gold leaf and freehand bronze painted on a wide band. The worn parts are outlined in white ink. *b.* A piece of frosted acetate is cut to fit the tray and fastened with masking tape to the floor of the tray through two holes cut in the acetate. The edge is left free for lifting and study-

7. When the design is an original one-piece stencil, next cut a piece of architect's linen to fit the perfected design, allowing an inch all around the edge. Place the linen over the drawing and fasten it at the corners with masking tape. Trace the design on the linen with a pen and India ink.

When the design is a composite stencil, it is necessary to make a separate drawing of each unit and to complete the drawing of any leaf or flower which partially fades off into the background. When an identical unit is repeated or reversed, only one drawing is necessary, except when two identical silhouette units are placed close together. Correct each drawing until the units make a perfect connection when stenciled. Cut a piece of linen to fit each separate unit, allowing an inch margin all around each edge. Place a piece of linen on each drawing and fasten it at the corners with masking tape. Trace the pattern on the linen with a pen and India ink.

44

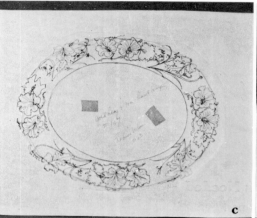

c

d

ing the design while it is being copied onto the acetate. The pen used is a Rapidograph #00. *c*. The complete copy is fastened to a piece of white cardboard through the center holes. *d*. The perfected ink drawing is made on a piece of fine tracing paper placed over the original drawing and fastened at the corners with masking tape.

Further Suggestions

Never get a drop of water or ammonia on the linen as it removes the sizing. This causes the linen to become wrinkled, and therefore useless. If a mistake is made in copying the design on the linen, it can be corrected with sepia ink in order to avoid wasting the piece of linen.

Keep linen flat at all times; do not roll it.

45

SECOND PROCESS

Cutting the Stencil

Materials Needed

Stencil traced on architect's linen
Piece of glass about 8″ × 10″, edges bound with masking tape
Steel-back razor blades (Gem) or Grifhold all-purpose knife
    #119, with Christy surgical blades #11
Stencil scissors, straight and curved
Clear nail polish
Hard Arkansas oil stone
Pliers
Table lamp with strong light
Magnifying glass or glasses for close work
Rubber dam punch, for punching small holes
Revolving leather punch, for punching larger holes

Procedure

1. Find the center of the flowers and punch all holes first. Insert a paper between the linen and the copper plate when using the leather punch.

2. Place the linen with the shiny side up on a piece of glass.

3. With the point of a razor blade or surgical knife, cut on the line, turning the linen with the left hand.

4. Refine and curve the edges with scissors if necessary.

Further Suggestions

By placing the linen on the glass with the shiny side up, it is

46

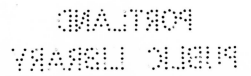

PLATE 10. Cutting a stencil. *a*. The razor blade is held steady with the right hand while the linen is turned slowly with the left hand. The point of the blade must be kept very sharp by sharpening it often on a fine oilstone. *b*. A stencil is cut with a Grifhold #119 knife with a Christy surgical blade inserted. The knife should be held quite straight. The point must be sharpened on an oilstone.

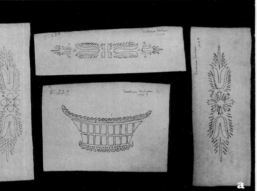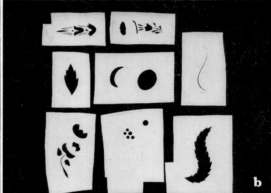

PLATE 11. Composite stencil. *a*. Ink tracings on linen before they have been cut. Each stencil is numbered. Name and date are written in the corner. *b*. Balance of units that have been cut out. The center unit in the bottom row is only partially cut out. *c*. These are the many units, cut out, which it takes to execute the elaborate composite pattern for an oblong stenciled tray. The tray stenciled with these units is pictured in PLATE 2, upper right.

PLATE 12. One-piece stencil. Notice the space of linen or "bridge" surrounding each cut-out unit. These later stencils could be produced much more quickly than the earlier composite stencils.

easier to follow the lines. The point of the razor blade must be kept very sharp. Moisten the oil stone and sharpen the blade often. When the point becomes rounded, break off the end of the blade with pliers and continue with the new point. Keep breaking off the end as long as the blade can be used for cutting. Very little pressure on the blade is needed if the blade is sufficiently sharp. When the blade begins to pull the linen, sharpen it or break off a new point. Some people prefer to cut with a Grifhold knife #119 into which a surgical blade can be inserted. Points and ragged lines may be corrected with stencil scissors, but great care must be taken not to stretch, roll, or wrinkle the linen. Always keep it flat. If the linen should become wrinkled, it can be pressed with a lukewarm iron—not a steam iron. If by mistake you cut through a stencil, it may be mended by cutting a thin sliver of linen, adding a drop of clear nail polish to the part to be mended, laying the sliver across the cut, and allowing it to dry untouched. When dry, recut with scissors if necessary. It is best to take your time and not make mistakes!

Do not be discouraged if your first stencil is not perfect. With a little practice you can master this skill in a short time. You will see an improvement with each stencil you cut; so have a little patience and you will be rewarded.

48

PLATE 13. Composite design copied from center slat of a Hitchcock chair.

PLATE 14. Composite design made up of many units and adaptable to any shape.

PLATE 15. One-piece stencil copied from a document box.

49

THIRD PROCESS

Application of the Stencil

Materials Needed

Cut-out stencil
Black Hazencote paper or Dura-Glo
Varnish, Pratt and Lambert, #61
Bronze powders
Velour palette
Velvet fingers, one for each shade of bronze powder, $4\frac{1}{2}''$ square. Velvet bobs
Old nylon stocking, cut in three equal pieces
Sponge cloth
Turpentine
Soft pencil eraser
Metal erasing shield
Bottle of carbon tetrachloride, Carbona, or Renuzit
Old cotton rags
Newspapers and wrapping paper
Piece of cardboard
Gold and white pencils
Varnish brush hung in baby bottle with turpentine
Masking tape
Box, drawer, or dust-proof closet large enough to hold wet stencil

Preparation of the Velour Palette

Hem or bind the edges of a piece of cotton-backed velour

50

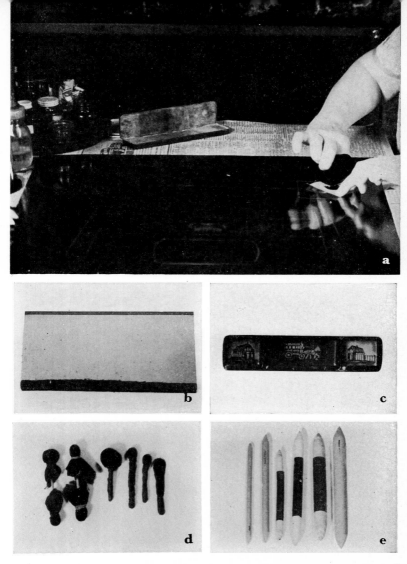

PLATE 16. Preparation of velour palette. *a.* A child's paint box is used as a palette for bronze powders. *b.* Velour palette, closed, showing cardboard backing and strip of velour left in center for arranging bronze powders. *c.* Child's paint box, closed, which is lined with velour for carrying in work kit. *d.* Velvet bobs made with silk-backed velvet wrapped around a Q-Tip or velvet stuffed with cotton. The size is varied by the amount of cotton used. *e.* French chamois stumps and charcoal stumps used for freehand bronzing.

51

about 12×14 inches. A strip of stiff cardboard may be pasted on either side of the back, leaving a space of two to three inches in the center for arranging the powders. A child's paintbox lined with velour makes a convenient palette to carry in your kit. In the center of the palette, arrange the bronze powders in the following order:

Smooth butler's silver
Antique silver
Rich gold
Pale gold
Antique gold
Belvedere
Orange Schliff
Copper
Fire bronze
Statuary
Patent green (seldom used)
Close the palette until ready for use.

Preparation of the Velvet Fingers and Bobs

Cut four-and-a-half-inch squares of silk-backed velvet, one for each shade of bronze powder. Hem the raw edges to prevent the loose threads from getting into the sticky varnish. To make bobs, wrap small pieces of velvet around Q-Tips and hold them in place with elastic bands. Different sizes of bobs can be made by increasing the amount of cotton. These bobs are used for freehand bronzing.

Procedure

How to Make the Pattern

1. Make a pattern out of wrapping paper to fit the chair, tray, or object to be decorated.

2. Mount black Hazencote paper on a piece of cardboard. To mount something, fasten it onto the cardboard on all four sides with masking tape. Dura-glo, which requires no mounting,

52

may be used instead. Lay the paper pattern on the black paper and outline the pattern with a white pencil.

3. Find the center, sides, and ends of the black paper pattern and mark these with a gold or white pencil.

4. Pour a small amount of varnish on the black paper pattern. Wad a piece of nylon stocking into a ball. Taking long strokes, rub the varnish quickly. Then crosshatch. Add varnish as needed, making sure that every part is covered, leaving no blobs. Fold the stocking into wax paper and save it for erasing mistakes.

5. Place the pattern in a box or dust-free drawer until it is sticky. In about fifteen to thirty minutes test it with a piece of linen. If the linen adheres but does not make a mark on the paper, the pattern is ready to be stenciled.

6. If the design is a composite one, start with the foremost unit and lay the stencil on the tacky varnish in proper position. If it is a one-piece stencil, center it and lay it on the varnish. Do not shift the stencil around.

7. Lay a piece of linen over the stencil and press around the edges of the cut-out part of the design until every edge adheres. Be careful not to touch the varnished surface with the fingers.

8. Open the velour palette, which has been prepared according to the instructions above, and place it on the right hand side on the work table. Wrap a piece of velvet around the forefinger, using a separate piece for each shade, and lightly dip into the bronze powder on the palette. Put the powder on the back of your left hand. Then start rubbing in a back and forth motion on the edge of the stencil. Pick up more powder from the back of your hand as needed. Polish the highlights and blend into the background. In the composite pattern, the stencils must not be overlapping or touching. It is imperative to leave the blended shadow surrounding each unit. If a stencil is reversed, be sure to clean it thoroughly with cleaning fluid on both sides before reversing it. If too much powder is used, it will creep under the stencil and leave a fuzzy edge which is difficult to correct. Mistakes can be rubbed out at this point with varnish and a nylon stocking without spoiling the background.

53

9. Leaves in early stencils were modelled by cutting a double curve (slender S-shape) on the edge of a piece of linen. Place the cut-out leaf on the tacky varnish. Find the edge of the S-curve which follows the midrib of the leaf and lay it on the leaf from the stem to the tip of the leaf. Rub the edge lightly with a velvet finger. Continue moving the S-curve around to form the finer veins, according to the growth of the leaf. Do not cross the midrib. When all the veins are modelled, blend the bronze powder into the edges and polish the tips of the leaf before removing the stencil. After 1825 a quicker process was used in which the veins were cut out of a single piece of linen. Place the cut-out veins in the center of the leaf, following the growth of the leaf, and rub firmly with a velvet finger. Remove the stencil and blend the bronze powders around the edge of the leaf leaving the space black around the veins. Polish the tips of the leaf before removing the leaf stencil.

The following examples show some of the various methods of veining leaves. Leaves stenciled in silhouette were often veined by adding freehand brush strokes later. Frequently the centers were filled in by freehand bronze and the brush strokes painted over the bronze.

PLATE 17. Modeled leaves with veining shaded by use of an S curve cut along the side of a piece of linen.

PLATE 18. Leaves with veins cut out in a piece of linen.

PLATE 19. Various methods of veining leaves; silhouette leaf.

PLATE 20. Various methods of veining leaves; silhouette leaves.

55

10. Never leave your stencils over night without cleaning them. Every time you finish stenciling, clean the stencils on both sides with a clean cotton cloth dampened with cleaning fluid. If the design is not completed in one process, allow twenty-four hours for it to dry. Then wash off with a dampened sponge cloth any excess powder which may not have become imbedded in the sticky varnish. Finger prints or excess powder on the background may be cleaned off with the addition of a little Lava soap. Mistakes within the pattern may be corrected by finding the proper curve on an erasing shield and placing it over the part to be corrected. Erase with a Pink Pearl soft pencil eraser #400. Replace cleaned stencils in a wax paper folder for future use. If the stencils are properly cleaned, they can be used many times.

11. Write your name, date, and number of pattern on the back of the cardboard or Dura-glo.

12. When the pattern is finished and has dried for twenty-four hours, protect it with a coat of varnish. When it is bone dry, cover it with clear acetate.

How to Apply the Stencil to the Article

The article to be stenciled should be prepared according to the instructions in "Preparation of Various Backgrounds" on pp. 32–34.

1. With a special brush used for varnish only, apply an even coat of varnish according to the previous directions. Do not apply it with a nylon stocking as was done for the pattern.

2. The length of time it takes varnish to dry to the proper stickiness varies according to the atmosphere. Usually allow forty-five minutes to an hour for Pratt and Lambert #61. Test the varnish with a piece of linen. When the linen adheres to the surface but does not leave an imprint on the varnished surface, it is time to begin stenciling.

3. Refer to the pattern, which was stenciled on the black paper, as a guide and proceed to apply the design in exactly the same way.

4. In twenty-four hours, wash off all the excess powder with a sponge cloth dampened in water. Clean any finger prints or

56

PLATE 21. Stenciling. *a*. Units of composite stencil cut out of architect's linen. *b*. Applying cut-out units on tacky varnished surface with velvet square wrapped around forefinger. *c*. Close-up view of composite stencil and velvet-wrapped forefinger in process of applying bronze powders. *d*. Stenciling a one-piece unit. No shading can be left surrounding the units. Notice the open child's paint box which is lined with velour and used as a palette.

57

smudges from the background with Lava soap but be careful not to rub over the stencil with Lava soap because it will remove the stencil. Make any necessary corrections on the stencil with a soft pencil eraser and a metal typewriter erasing shield. Find a curve to fit the area to be corrected and lay it on carefully in order not to scratch the stencil. Erase. Mistakes can also be painted out with a fine brush, using the same paint mixture that was used on the background. If the stencil was not placed in the proper position or if mistakes become too difficult to repair, wash the entire stencil off with Lava soap mixed with a little dental pumice. Dry. Revarnish and stencil again. When the powders no longer are absorbed into the tacky varnish, they take on a metallic look. Then it is time to stop stenciling.

5. In twenty-four hours, wash off the excess powder and correct mistakes. Revarnish and continue to stencil. Stencils can be placed over the previous stencils and polished again if so desired. This process may be repeated as many times as necessary to complete the pattern. When replacing a stencil, extreme accuracy is necessary to avoid a double line.

6. When all the stenciling is finished, dried for twenty-four hours, and corrections made, finish according to directions under Final Varnish Finish, pp. 39–40. Striping may be done on the second coat of varnish which has been rubbed smooth.

58

FOURTH PROCESS
Striping

Materials Needed

Sword striper 00
Scroller for small articles
Media:
  Varnish
  Nobles & Hoare quick-drying gold size
  Lowe Bros. Co. tulip yellow plax #826 or Giles black seal
  Any desired japan color paint thinned with medium
Turpentine
Cleaning fluid
Glossy magazine
Tin lid for mixing paint (tins from the end of frozen fruits
  are ideal)
Rags
Practice pad

How to Make a Practice Pad

Mount a cardboard with black paper, attaching it with masking tape on all four sides. Dura-glo, which requires no mounting, may be used instead. Varnish. Dry for twenty-four hours.
Practice striping, clean it off, and repeat.

Procedure

1. Mark the stripe with a pencil. Put bronze powder or paint
in a long narrow tin. Add the medium and mix it well with a

PLATE 22. How to stripe the flange of a tray. *a.* Position of brush while striping. Notice how the short handle is held in the palm of the hand by the thumb and first finger. The last three fingers rest firmly on the surface to act as a guide. *b.* Striping the flange of a tray with the last three fingers locked over the edge. The glove, with thumb and fore-finger cut out, helps the hand to slide along the varnished surface.

60

palette knife. The consistency should be thin enough for the mixture to flow out of the brush and yet cover the newsprint of a magazine.

2. Load the striping brush and stroke it back and forth on a glossy magazine until the mixture is well distributed in the brush. Do not leave a blob of paint near the end of the brush.

3. Hold the short handle of the brush between the thumb and forefinger. Lay the brush on the previously marked stripe and pull the brush toward you, using the last three fingers as a guide. When striping a tray, however, lock the last three fingers around the flange of the tray. (It helps the hand to slide along the varnished surface if you wear an old glove out of which the thumb and first finger have been cut.) The width of the stripe varies according to the amount of pressure on the brush. Do not lay the brush down beyond the chiseled hairs. For a very wide stripe quickly run the brush along one side and then the other and fill in between the two lines before the paint has a chance to settle. If it is necessary to stop before the stripe is completed, always start about an inch back in the stripe. Do not look back where you have been but look where you are going. Move the brush along slowly at the same rate of speed.

4. Corrections should be made immediately. Stretch a lint-free cloth, slightly dampened with cleaning fluid, over a finger and quickly run it along the edge of the stripe. Corrections can also be made the next day by painting along the edges with the same background color.

5. A more brilliant or solid bronze stripe may be made by rubbing the painted stripe with bronze powder. Use a velvet finger when the proper stickiness has been reached. In twenty-four hours wash off the excess powder.

6. It may be necessary for a beginner to remove the stripe several times before satisfactory results are obtained. Remove the stripe with cleaning fluid and a lint-free cloth. When the striping mixture becomes thick and gummy and will not flow

from the brush evenly, discard it. Make a new mixture, clean the brush in turpentine, and try again.

Further Suggestions

All striping must be done on a varnished surface which has been rubbed to a smooth dull finish. The color should contrast with the background, usually a light color on a dark background and black or a dark color on a light background. A bronze stripe may be used alone or in addition to a stripe of any color.

Striping is a technique which takes much practice to master. All decorated tin or wood must be striped to achieve the final finishing touch.

FIFTH PROCESS
Tinting the Stencil

Materials Needed

Design stenciled on black paper protected with one coat of
   varnish dried twenty-four hours
Small tubes of artist's oil paint:
   Transparent colors
      Alizarin crimson
      Prussian blue
      Indian yellow or yellow lake
   Semi-transparent colors
      Raw umber
      Burnt umber
      Burnt sienna
Assortment of square-tipped French quill brushes. Art &
   Sign, series ♯474 or ♯475, sizes 0 through 8. (See directions
   below for Inserting Handles)
Wooden handles for brushes
Sable water color brush ♯1 or spotter ♯00 for clean up
Paint palette or a white tile
Palette knife
Nobles and Hoare quick-drying gold size, used as medium
Lard oil or Neatsfoot oil
Small bottle of cleaning fluid
Small bottle of turpentine
Cotton rags

Bottle caps, small screw type
Tube of Le Page's liquid solder
Glossy magazine

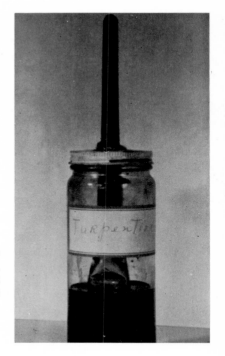

PLATE 23. Care of the brush. Olive jar with hole cut out of metal screw top. A paint brush is inserted in the hole. The turpentine must be kept just above the ferrule.

Directions for Inserting Handles
in Quill Brushes

Soak the quill brushes in hot water until the quill becomes soft. In the meantime, as quill brushes do not come equipped with handles, file a wooden handle to fit and insert it while the quill is soft. When the proper fit is achieved, add a drop of Le Page's liquid solder and work the handle down to the hairs. French quill brushes are used after the paint is thinned with a medium to cause the brush stroke to settle-out smooth and not show any ridges; they are also used for most country painting.

Care of Paint Brushes

Clean the brush in a jar of turpentine and squeeze the hairs several times in a lint-free cloth or paper toweling. Then dip

64

the brush into cleaning fluid and wipe it until no paint remains in the brush. Dip the hairs, up to the ferrule, into lard oil, Neatsfoot oil, or Stat and squeeze them out between the fingers. Lay the brush straight in a dust-free box until it is needed. Remember to clean it thoroughly in turpentine before using it again.

Procedure

How to Make the Pattern

1. Spread newspaper over the work table. Place the paint palette on the right. Open a glossy magazine to a clean dust-free page on which to strike the brush (called dressing the brush). Fill one bottle cap with medium and another with turpentine.

2. Squeeze a small amount of oil paint onto the palette. On one side place the alizarin crimson, the burnt umber, and then the transparent yellow. On the opposite side place the Prussian blue near the raw umber.

3. With a palette knife pick up a small amount of alizarin crimson, add a little burnt umber, and blend it with enough medium to produce a flowing consistency. Mix Prussian blue and raw umber in the same manner. A variety of shades of green can be obtained by varying the proportions of blue and yellow with raw umber.

4. If the brush has been oiled, clean it with turpentine and wipe it dry with a cloth before starting to paint.

5. Load the French quill brush with the medium. Dress the brush on the magazine in order to distribute the medium and arrange the hairs in the proper position. Then pick up the desired color on one edge of the brush and make one continuous stroke. Control the brush in such a way that the edge of the brush loaded with the paint will leave the dark shadow where desired. The color in the brush will blend with the medium in the brush and fade out to light or nothing along the edge. Allow a few minutes for it to settle. If the proper effect is not achieved, wipe the paint off with varnish and try again. Hold the brush up straight and swing it in a circular motion, painting right over

65

the black sections since the transparent mixture will not show over the black. Alizarin crimson is usually floated over the gold and Prussian blue over the silver. Often a little of the gold or silver is allowed to show at the edges.

6. In twenty-four hours a coat of varnish should be applied before continuing with further decoration.

How to Apply the Tint to the Article

1. When the applied stencil has been corrected and cleaned, apply a coat of varnish. Dry twenty-four hours. Varnish again. Dry twenty-four hours. Rub the surface lightly with Lava soap and pumice. Wash, dry, and varnish it again. Rub the stencil to a smooth dull finish with wet or dry sandpaper.

2. Proceed with the same technique as used on the pattern. Transparent brush strokes can be removed with cleaning fluid and applied over and over again since the three coats of varnish provide a good protective coat over the stencil.

SIXTH PROCESS
Freehand Brush Strokes

Materials Needed

Selection of French quill brushes. Art & Sign, series #474 or
  #475, sizes 0 through 8
Sable scroller #1 or #2, Art & Sign or Grumbacher
Small water color brush or spotter
Artist oil paints, small tubes:
  Transparent colors
    Alizarin crimson
    Prussian blue
    Indian yellow or yellow lake
  Semi-transparent colors
    Raw umber
    Burnt umber
    Burnt sienna
    Yellow ochre
    Titanium white
  Japan colors
    Sign Craft red, made by the T. J. Roman Paint Corp.
    Venetian red
    Chrome yellow, medium
    Striping white
Practice pad
Paint palette
Cleaning fluid

Turpentine
Small bottle of asphaltum
Nobles & Hoare quick-drying gold size
Palette knife
Lard oil, Neatsfoot oil, or Stat
Cotton rags
Small bottle caps
Glossy magazine
Tube of Le Page's liquid solder
Wooden handles for brushes

Paint Mixtures Used in Early American Decoration

Transparent mixtures, thinned with varnish or Nobles & Hoare quick-drying gold size as a medium

Red
: Alizarin crimson
: Sometimes burnt umber, Indian yellow, or Prussian blue

Blue
: Prussian blue
: Raw umber

Yellow
: Indian yellow or yellow lake
: Raw umber
: Prussian blue

Green
: Indian yellow or yellow lake
: Raw umber

White
: Titanium white
: Medium

Opaque mixtures, thinned with varnish or Nobles & Hoare quick-drying gold size used as a medium

Red
: Sign Craft red (japan)
: Sometimes burnt umber

Country Green
: Chrome yellow medium (japan)
: Prussian blue
: Raw umber

68

"Dirty"
Yellow
$\left\{\begin{array}{l}\text{Chrome yellow medium (japan)}\\\text{Few drops of asphaltum mixed}\\\quad\text{with medium in a bottle cap}\end{array}\right.$

"Dirty"
white
$\left\{\begin{array}{l}\text{Striping white}\\\text{Few drops of asphaltum mixed}\\\quad\text{with medium in a bottle cap}\\\text{Sometimes a little yellow ochre}\end{array}\right.$

Mixtures for lace-edge painting will be included in that process, p. 99.

Procedure

1. Prepare a work table as described in "Tinting the Stencil," p. 63.

2. Squeeze a small amount of paint colors onto the palette according to the mixture desired.

3. Fill a bottle cap with medium. Fill a small container with turpentine for cleaning the brushes. Place these near the palette.

4. Place a glossy magazine on which to dress the brush on the right of the work table.

5. With the palette knife, lift a small amount of paint squeezed from the tube and mix it thoroughly with medium on the palette. Add more pigment or medium as needed.

6. For the "dirty" white and "dirty" yellow, the procedure is different. Add a few drops of asphaltum to the medium and mix this with the color on the palette. Asphaltum is semi-transparent and therefore helps to give the desired effect of thick and thin brush strokes. The asphaltum replaces the umbers often used.

7. When using japan colors, they must be applied immediately due to the quick-drying agency. A lid placed over the mixture when it is not in use will slow down the drying process.

8. Select the largest quill brush possible to make the least number of strokes. If it is necessary to make more than one stroke, first stroke on one side, then the other, and fill in the center.

69

9. Load the brush with the mixture and stroke the brush back and forth several times on the magazine. This distributes the paint and arranges the brush hairs in the proper position to form a thin knife-like edge. The stroke may be started with the knife-like side or the widened side.

10. There are three basic brush strokes to master.

    a. Lay the flat side of the brush on the surface, rest it there for a brief instant, and then press forward slightly before you swing the brush to the right or left. At the same time as you swing the brush, turn it in such a way that the hairs will fall back into position to make the fine tail.

    b. Start with the knife-like edge of the brush, press in the middle, and end with a fine hairline.

    c. Start with the wide end, press forward slightly, and then pull the brush straight down, slowly releasing to end in a fine point, called a "tear drop."

These are attained by the pressure and release of the brush.

11. Hold the loaded brush perpendicular and press to make a blob. Start moving the brush toward you with a rolling motion, releasing the pressure to bring the hairs into the proper knife-like position necessary to make a thin tail. If the brush has not been properly dressed, too much paint will remain, and it will be impossible to achieve a fine tail. When the paint refuses to flow out of the brush, the mixture has become too thick and gummy. The brush should then be cleaned and a fresh mixture prepared.

12. A scroller is a brush with long hairs which taper to a fine point. One type is made of sable hairs which have considerable resilience. To make a scroll with this type of brush, the brush must be held perpendicular in the hand. However, it must be held freely so that a continuous circular motion can be made while the brush is gradually pressed and released at each turn.

70

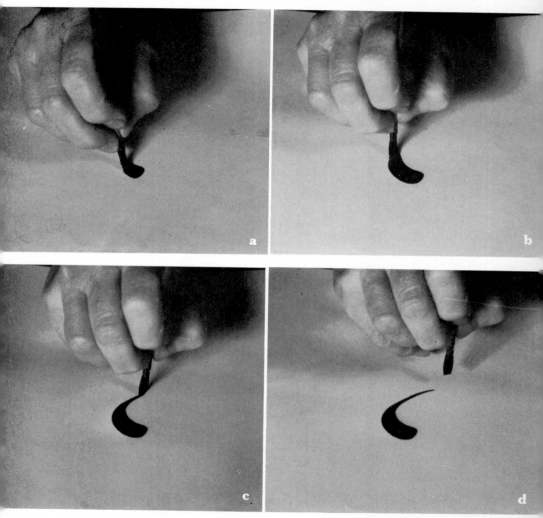

24. Brush strokes. *a*. Beginning of brush stroke made with flat side of square-tipped quill brush made from camel hair. *b*. Brush gradually swings right while it is pressed and turned to arrange hairs in proper position to make a fine tail. *c*. Position of hairs in brush when making a long, thin tail. *d*. Completed brush stroke.

71

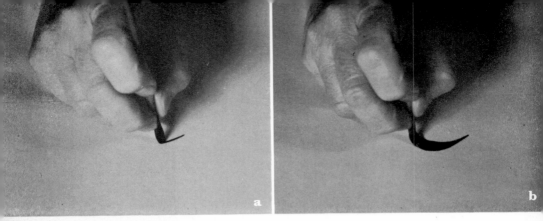

PLATE 25. Brush strokes. *a*. Position of hairs in square-tipped quill brush when beginning brush stroke with a knifelike edge. *b*. A slight pressure is applied while gradually swinging brush to right. *c*. Brush is turned to left as pressure is released, and hairs arrange themselves to finish with a thin, fine tail. *d*. Position of hairs in brush when ending with a fine hair line. *e*. Completed brush stroke.

PLATE 26. Brush strokes. *a*. Beginning of brush stroke made with flat side of square-tipped quill brush—before starting downward to make what is called a teardrop stroke. *b*. Downward movement as brush is turned and pressure released to end with a long, thin tail. *c*. Position of brush hairs in knifelike edge to end stroke in a fine point.

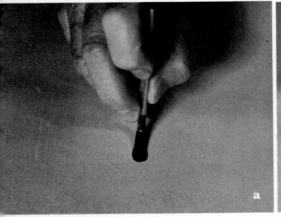

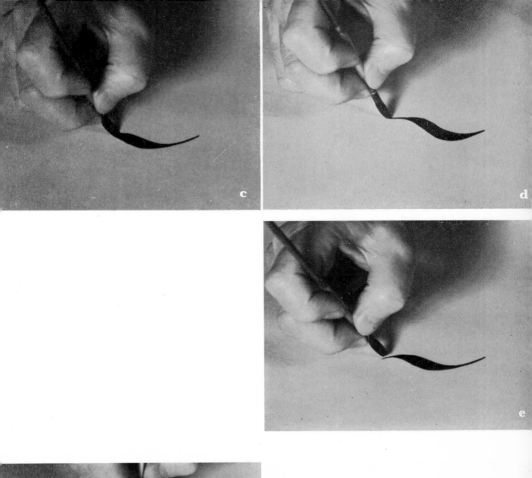

PLATE 27. Basic brush strokes.

74

◀ PLATE 28. Freehand brush strokes.

75

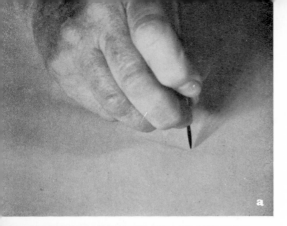

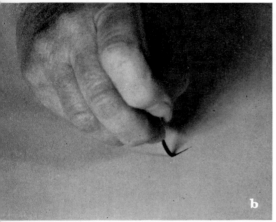

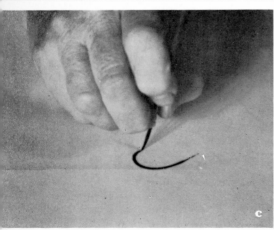

PLATE 29. Use of the sable scroller. *a*. Position of brush when beginning a scroll with a sable scroller. *b*. Slight pressure is applied as brush begins to rotate in circular motion. *c*. Continuation of scroll through use of circular motion and slight pressure.

PLATE 30. Scroll made with a sable scroller.

SEVENTH PROCESS
Country Painting

Materials Needed

All the materials listed under "Freehand Brush Strokes" on
    p. 67–68.
Frosted and clear acetate
Fine tracing paper
Lithopone or cake of magnesium carbonate
Graphite paper
Masking tape
Stylus
Crow quill pen
India ink
Turpentine
Cleaning fluid
Rags
Chalk paper

How to Make a Chalk Paper

Cut a piece of tracing paper about 6 × 8 inches. Rub turpentine into the paper with a cloth. Let it dry for a few minutes. With the fingers, work lithopone or magnesium into the damp paper. Work this all the way to the edges and shake off the excess powder. Fold the paper, chalk side in, and write on the back "chalk paper." Keep this in your kit for tracing patterns on dark backgrounds. For light backgrounds, make chalk paper with pastel chalks for each transparent color used. Graphite paper may be used for light backgrounds, but it is very difficult to cover unless the paint mixture is opaque.

Procedure

How to Make the Pattern

1. Fasten a piece of tracing paper over the design and make a tracing with a crow quill pen and India ink. It is not necessary to copy the transparent over-strokes. These are painted in later, freehand.

If the design to be copied is an old original piece, follow the instructions given in "Tracing a Stencil Pattern" #6, p. 43.

2. Remove the tracing and fasten it on a cardboard with masking tape.

3. Cut a piece of frosted acetate large enough to fit over the design and leave enough margin for striping and mounting later. Fasten the acetate over the tracing, dull side up, at the corners only. This will leave enough room to slip a piece of black paper under the acetate to test the colour while you are painting.

4. Prepare a work table as described in "Tinting the Stencil" #1, p. 65. Fill a bottle cap with medium. Fill a small container with turpentine for cleaning the brushes.

5. Mix the base colors of the design according to the directions in "Freehand Brush Strokes" p. 68–69 under Opaque Mixtures. Use only enough medium to spread the paint flat and smooth. Japan colors are opaque but become semi-transparent if they are mixed with too much varnish.

6. Select the largest quill brush possible and paint the base colors according to the instructions in "Freehand Brush Strokes" pp. 70–77. Test the colors by slipping a piece of black paper between the tracing and the acetate. Typical of country painting is a base foundation of an opaque color with superimposed transparent brush strokes to complete the form. Let the under coat dry for twenty-four hours and then protect it with a coat of varnish. Let this dry for twenty-four hours.

7. The next day paint the freehand brush strokes and the super-imposed transparent brush strokes. Mix the colors according to "Freehand Brush strokes" p. 68 under Transparent Mixtures. If the brush stroke does not give the desired effect, wipe it out with a cloth and cleaning fluid and repeat. A color which touches another cannot be painted until the first color is thoroughly dry. Dry for twenty-four hours and then varnish.

8. Paint in all the fine black lines and scrolls with a scroller and Giles black seal or India ink. It is advisable but not necessary to protect all painting with a coat of varnish before applying the fine black lines. This gives an added protection for cleaning off brush strokes and repeating whenever necessary.

9. Stripe. Dry twenty-four hours. Varnish. Dry.

10. Mount the design on a black background. When it is bone dry, cover it with clear acetate for protection. Leave one end open for air space.

How to Apply the Design to the Article

1. Fasten the original pen and ink tracing to the article at each corner only, making sure it is properly centered. Slip the chalk paper, chalk side down, under the tracing paper. With a stylus, transfer the design to the background, moving the chalk paper around underneath the design. This will leave a fine white impression of the design to be painted. Do not copy super-imposed brush strokes.

2. Using the design on the pattern as a model, follow this pattern when painting the design on the article.

3. When all the decorating and striping is finished and has dried for twenty-four hours, proceed with the final finish described in "Backgrounds" p. 39–40.

80

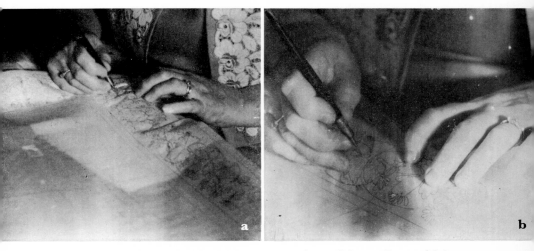

PLATE 31. How to transfer the design to the article. *a*. Pen-and-ink drawing being transferred from tracing paper to flange of a tray. The chalk paper is slipped under the tracing paper with the chalk side next to the tray. *b*. Tracing design onto tray with a stylus. *c*. Tracing a stripe onto the tray by holding a ruler firmly with the left hand and sliding the right hand, with stylus, along the edge. *d*. Tracing paper is turned back, showing portion of design transferred to flange of tray.

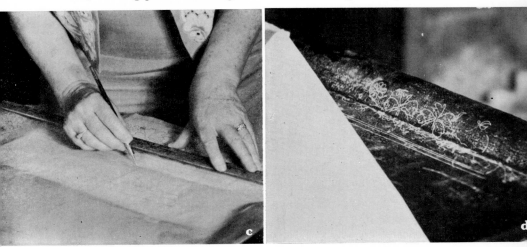

81

EIGHTH PROCESS

Freehand Bronze

Materials Needed

Frosted and clear acetate
Tracing paper
Selection of bronze powders
Selection of French quill brushes. Art & Sign, series #474 or
    #475, sizes 0 through 8
Scroller. Art & Sign, series #831, sizes 1 and 2
Brights sable brushes. Art & Sign, series #823, sizes 2 and 4
Velvet squares, silk-backed
Velvet bobs
Charcoal stumps
Etching needle
Velour palette
Giles black seal or japan colors mixed with medium
Cleaning fluid
Sponge cloth
Glossy magazine

Procedure

How to Make the Pattern

1. Make a pen and ink tracing of the design. Mount the tracing on cardboard. Cut a piece of frosted acetate large enough to cover the design and fasten this, dull side up, over the tracing at each corner.

Plate 32. Painting a freehand bronze design. *a.* Freehand bronze design is painted on a piece of frosted acetate. The design, traced in ink on tracing paper, is mounted at the corners with masking tape, and the frosted acetate is placed over the drawing and fastened at the corners with masking tape. *b.* A bob is used to work the bronze powders into the tacky black varnish. In this picture, a stencil is also used to form a sharp edge.

Plate 33. Example of a design painted in freehand bronze.

2. Pour a small amount of Giles black seal into a bottle cap. Freehand bronzing is often done in red or green. Mix the japan color with medium to the proper shade and consistency.

3. Select the proper square-tipped French quill brush and paint directly on the frosted acetate. Spread the hairs in the brush and complete in one brush stroke whenever possible. Painting should be smooth and even. Accuracy is important since it is almost impossible to make corrections. Any stickiness remaining on the background from the corrections will also receive the bronze powder.

4. When the paint is almost dry, start working in the bronze powders with a bob or brush according to the pattern. For a fine sharp edge, use a charcoal stump or a brights sable brush, dampened with saliva. Blend the powders out, starting from the highlight. The painting medium should be dry enough for the velvet to create a "squeak." If the painting is too wet, it will not take the necessary polish and blend. Sometimes a stencil is combined with freehand bronzing to form a pattern. There is much more freedom with freehand bronzing than with stenciling, but freehand bronzing is often mistaken for stenciling.

5. In twenty-four hours, wash off the excess powders with a damp sponge cloth. If too much powder was embedded in certain places, it may be lifted out by adding a little Lava soap to the damp sponge cloth. Remove any finger prints from the background with Lava soap or cleaning fluid. Varnish.

6. In twenty-four hours a transparent wash may be added if desired.

7. In another twenty-four hours any freehand brush strokes may be added.

8. In twenty-four hours varnish.

How to Apply the Design to the Article

1. Place the tracing paper with the design traced in ink in the correct position on the article. Slip chalk paper under the tracing and mark the design on the background with a stylus.

A fine white line will outline the design to be painted. Remove the tracing.

2. Paint freehand on the article in exactly the same way as described directly above in How to Make a Pattern. Continue the process until the design is completed.

Usually freehand bronze designs are painted on light colored backgrounds. When painted on a black background, the powder must be extended to the edge of the painting. If the design is painted in a contrasting color, do not bring the powder to the edge but leave the tips showing.

3. In twenty-four hours varnish. Finish the article with varnish and striping as described in the earlier process.

NINTH PROCESS
Gold Leaf

Materials Needed

Book of 23-karat gold leaf, loose or mounted
Gold bronze powder
French quill brushes
Sable scroller
Spotter, for fine brush strokes and clean up
Nobles and Hoare quick-drying gold size or a slow-drying oil
    size
Japan chrome yellow
Yellow plax
Gold bronze powder
Giles black seal
Paint palette
Frosted acetate
Velvet squares
Velour palette
Cleaning fluid
Etching needle
Grifhold Stencil Knife #3, 1/16″ blade
Bowl point pen
Glossy magazine
Rags
Chalk paper
Masking tape

86

Wax paper, for picking up unmounted gold leaf
Soft camel's hair brush

Procedure

How to Make the Pattern

1. Make an ink tracing of the design on tracing paper.

2. Mount the tracing on cardboard, attatching it with masking tape. Cover the tracing with a piece of acetate, frosted side up. Fasten it at each corner with masking tape.

3. Pour turpentine into a small container for cleaning brushes. Pour a small amount of Giles black seal into a bottle cap. Open a dust-free page of a glossy magazine and place it on the right of the work table.

4. Select the largest square-tipped brush suitable to paint the largest area. Clean the brush in turpentine and wipe it dry. Load the brush with Giles black seal and work it back and forth on the magazine to distribute the black varnish and arrange the hairs in the brush. This is called "dressing the brush."

5. Paint the largest area first. Use as few brush strokes as possible. Quickly fill in the centers between brush strokes before the varnish has a chance to settle. Painting should dry very smooth and show no brush strokes. Change to smaller brushes when necessary. Very fine lines and scrolls are painted with a sable scroller, held perpendicular. Some fine lines may be drawn with a bowl point pen dipped in black seal.

6. When the design is completed, wipe off all finger prints from the background with a clean cloth and cleaning fluid.

7. Place the pattern in a dust-free place until the varnish reaches the proper stage for rubbing in the bronze powders. The length of time will depend upon the amount of humidity in the atmosphere.

8. Occasionally test the tips by rubbing in the gold bronze powder with a velvet square. When the proper stickiness has been reached, no threads will come out of the velvet, and the powder will take on a high polish. If the varnish gets too dry,

87

it will not accept the powder but will take on a metallic look. It is important to complete the pattern at the proper time. This will take a little experience. When the pattern is finished, let it dry for twenty-four hours.

9. The next day wash off all excess powder from the background with water and a sponge cloth. If necessary, use a little detergent. If the bronze powder is properly embedded into the varnish, it will not wash off. If the varnish was too dry, most of the powder will wash off. Since there is no way to correct this error, the entire design must be painted again if this happens.

10. Etching and corrections should be done within twenty-four hours, before the varnish dries too hard. Place the acetate on a piece of glass and etch with an etching needle according to the design. The edges can be refined by carefully scraping any excess off with a Grifhold Stencil Knife #3. Clean off the remaining particles with a little cotton wrapped on the end of a toothpick and dipped in cleaning fluid. Dry twenty-four hours.

11. Varnish over the entire pattern and let it dry for twenty-four hours.

12. Transparent painting may now be added. Mix the paint with Nobles & Hoare quick-drying gold size. Corrections of over-painting and freehand brush strokes can be made on the dry varnished surface without injuring the underneath painting by wiping off with varnish. Use cleaning fluid sparingly. Dry twenty-four hours.

13. The final freehand brush strokes, pen work, and striping may now be added to complete the pattern.

14. In twenty-four hours varnish the surface again to protect the design. Let it dry thoroughly and cover it with clear acetate.

How to Apply Gold Leaf to the Article

Prepare the background of the tin or wood article to be decorated according to the instructions in "Backgrounds," pp. 32–34. The final varnished surface should be bone-dry and rubbed to a smooth dull finish. Never lay gold leaf when the humidity is above 70%.

1. Rub talcum powder over the prepared surface and blow off any excess.

2. Place the ink drawing of the design in the proper position on the article. Fasten it with masking tape leaving room to slip the chalk paper underneath.

3. With the chalk side next to the surface, slip the chalk paper around under the tracing and trace with a stylus until the design is completed. Remove the tracing and the chalk paper.

4. Pour gold size into a small bottle cap and mix it thoroughly with a little japan chrome yellow, yellow plax, or gold bronze powder. The color is added to clarify the painting. Any contrasting color may be used, but the yellow or gold will show less through the pin holes, or "holidays" as they are called, left in the gold leaf.

5. Clean any stickiness and moisture from your hands and powder your hands and arms with talcum powder. Any moisture left on the background from finger prints or corrections will cause the gold leaf to stick. Keep the powder puff handy to keep your hands free of perspiration.

6. Select the proper square-tipped brush. Paint with gold size the largest units first using the same technique as described directly above in How to Make a Pattern.

7. Test the gold size with the tip of the little finger to judge when it is time to lay the gold leaf. The gold size should be almost dry but should still be sticky enough to hold the gold leaf. If the gold leaf is not mounted, prepare squares of wax paper. The workroom must be free from draughts. Open the book to a page of gold leaf, which is held between two pieces of rouge paper, and without breathing on the gold leaf, carefully place a square of wax paper over it. Rub the wax paper lightly until the gold leaf adheres. Transfer the gold leaf to the gold size and rub the wax paper lightly with the tips of the fingers until the gold leaf adheres to the painted surface. Remove the wax paper. Repeat this process until all the painted units are covered. Do not worry about the gold leaf which remains loose at the edges of the painting. This is brushed off later. It may be necessary to lay some

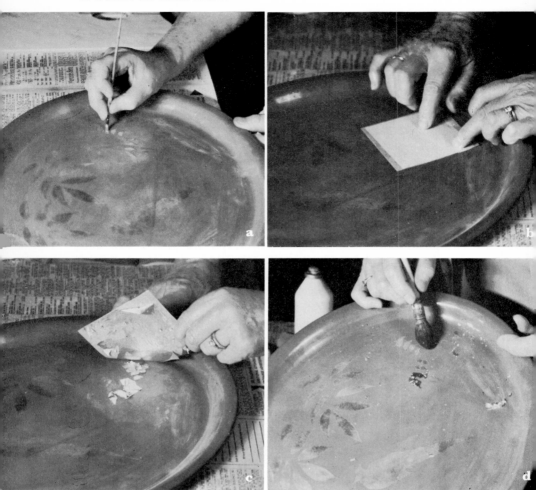

PLATE 34. How to lay gold leaf on tin or wood. *a.* Painting a gold-leaf design on a tray. A mixture of Nobles and Hoare gold size, mixed with a little japan chrome yellow, is painted on with a square-tipped quill brush. *b.* A sheet of mounted gold leaf is laid over the painted design and stroked lightly with the ball of the finger. *c.* The gold leaf adheres to the tacky painted design as the mounted gold leaf is re-moved. *d.* The extra gold leaf is brushed off with a very soft brush.

painted units before the design is completed. Small units and brush strokes dry quickly and may have to be layed almost immediately. The proper moment to lay gold leaf depends on a combination of several things, such as the length of drying time for the mixture used in painting, the distribution of the medium, and the humidity. The longer it takes for the medium to dry, the more shiny the gold leaf will be. When gold leaf is layed too soon, it becomes embedded in the medium and leaves a dull rough look.

8. In about an hour, brush off the excess gold leaf with a very soft camel's hair brush or a piece of fine cotton. Be careful not to scratch the gold leaf. Any rough particles in the cotton or particles of gold left in the brush or cotton will leave a scratch. Fill in any holidays with gold leaf immediately. The warmth

PLATE 35. Gold leaf applied to a tray. The tray has three coats of varnish applied over the gold leaf. The varnish is thoroughly dried and sanded to a smooth, dull finish. It is now ready for the application of transparent colors over the gold leaf and the addition of freehand brush strokes to complete the design.

91

of the finger will usually cause the gold leaf to adhere. If the gold leaf refuses to stick, try breathing on the gold leaf and laying it quickly.

9. Within twenty-four hours all the lines should be etched with an etching needle. Corrections should also be done at this time, before the gold size hardens. The edges can be scraped off and refined by using a Grifhold Stencil Knife #3. Clean off all particles of gold leaf which may have stuck to the background by scraping or by wiping with a toothpick wrapped in cotton and dipped in carbon tetrachloride. Mistakes can also be painted out with a little of the background paint and a small fine sable brush.

10. Allow the gold leaf to dry thoroughly for at least a week. Burnish it with a piece of cotton. Varnish. Dry twenty-four hours.

11. Transparent colors and freehand brush strokes can now be added to complete the pattern. Most gold leaf patterns have freehand brush strokes of umber or color. Allow twenty-four hours between each color, brush stroke, or pen work added on top of a previous color.

12. Stripe the article with gold leaf, a mixture of gold size, and bronze powder or a color suitable to the design and article.

13. Dry thoroughly. Varnish. Finish the surface according to the Final Varnish Finish, pp. 39–40 under "Backgrounds."

TENTH PROCESS
Floating Color

Materials Needed

French quill brushes. Art & Sign, series #484, sizes 0, 2, 4, 6, 8, and 10

M. Grumbacher, series #626B, sizes 2, 4, 6, 8, 10, and 12

M. Grumbacher, series #6661, $\frac{1}{4}''$ wide and all sizes

Show-card brushes *or* square-tipped sable brushes, Art & Sign, series #914, $\frac{1}{4}''$ wide

Square-tipped sable brush. Art & Sign, series #914, 3/8'' wide

Pointed water color brushes

Varnish or size

Linseed oil or slow size

Turpentine

Carbon tetrachloride

Tubes of artist's oil colors

Tube of japan striping white

Crow quill pen or Rapidograph fountain pen

India ink

Frosted acetate

Tracing paper

Paint palette

Glossy magazine

Bottle caps

Cardboard

Palette knife

Rags

Stylus
Wrapping paper

Procedure

How to Make the Pattern

1. Fasten a piece of tracing paper over the design to be copied. Copy the basic design with a crow quill pen and India ink. It is not necessary to trace the over-stroke painting. This is painted freehand.

2. Cover a piece of cardboard with black paper secured with masking tape or use a piece of Dura-glo. Make a pattern of the tray or article out of wrapping paper. Trace this pattern onto the black paper, marking the outline with a white pencil. Mount the India ink tracing of the design on the black paper in the proper position, and then cover this tracing with acetate, frosted side up and fasten down at the corners with masking tape.

3. Paint the gold-leaf border, drips, and underneath gold units first. Lay the gold leaf according to the previous instructions. Let the gold-leaf painting dry for twenty-four hours. Protect it with a coat of varnish which also must dry for twenty-four hours.

4. Fill a container with turpentine for cleaning the brushes. Fill a bottle cap with varnish or gold size. Place the paint palette and the glossy magazine to the right on the work table. Squeeze a small amount of striping white onto the palette. Using a palette knife, mix the varnish with the striping white on the palette. Load the quill brush and work it back and forth on the magazine. The mixture should be thin enough to leave the print readable.

5. Using a French quill brush, paint the basic form of the rose, flower, or bird with this thin mixture, over which the color is to be floated and which should settle out to a smooth and transparent undercoat. Allow to dry for twenty-four hours.

6. The next day, pour varnish or gold size into a jar lid and add a drop or two of linseed oil to slow the drying process. This is called slow varnish. If slow size is used, linseed oil is not

necessary. Too much oil will cause the paint to crawl. Use Grumbacher #6661 brush or a similar show-card brush and paint the exact basic form with slow varnish.

7. With a palette knife, mix umber or the color to be floated with slow varnish on a palette. Select the proper size sable water color brush or show-card brush and load it with the slow varnish. Stroke the brush back and forth on a glossy magazine. Then pick up the color from the palette on one side of the brush and quickly apply the brush to the basic form previously painted with slow varnish, guiding the loaded edge along the lines where the dark shadows would naturally fall. The color will fuse and blend off into the slow varnish as it settles. For example, when painting a rose, a dark shadow is floated into the center of the rose to form the inner rose, called the cup. Another dark shadow is floated along the base where the petals are attached to the rose, called the saucer. Shadows may also be floated along one edge of the petals following the growth of the rose. Allow the floating color to dry twenty-four hours. Discard any leftover varnish and paint mixture.

8. The next day, repeat the floating process, making a fresh mixture of slow varnish in a jar lid. Mix each transparent color to be floated with slow varnish on a separate spot on a palette, using a palette knife. Use Grumbacher's #6661 brush and paint the basic form with slow varnish only. Use a separate water color brush for each color. Load each brush with slow varnish and work back and forth on a glossy magazine before picking up the mixture of color and slow varnish from the palette on one side of the brush. Again float each color into the slow varnish which was painted over the basic form. With a square-tipped sable brush or a show-card brush, blend the colors from dark to light. This entire process must be done quickly before the varnish "sets up." It is often necessary to repeat this process several times before the desired effect is achieved. Allow twenty-four hours between each floating process. Always make a fresh mixture. Do not use any leftover paint mixture.

9. Freehand brush strokes may be added the next day to

95

accent the highlights and complete the form. Dry twenty-four hours.

10. The final touch is called "veiling." Make a thin mixture of striping white and varnish on the palette. Pick up paint on one side of a quill brush and outline the edges of the petals of the rose. Lift out the excess and blend the paint out to nothing, leaving a thin white edge on the petals. This effect simulates the bloom on the rose. Dry twenty-four hours.

11. When the paint is thoroughly dry, protect it with a coat of varnish. Dry twenty-four hours. Stripe. Dry. Mount the pattern on black cardboard and cover it with clear acetate.

PLATE 36. This illustration shows the ink drawing of the design on tracing paper fastened to the head tray with a piece of masking tape through a hole cut in the paper where there is no design. The chalk paper can be slipped under the edge of the tracing and traced onto the surface with a stylus.

How to Apply the Design to the Article

1. Prepare the background according to the previous instructions in "Backgrounds," pp. 32–34. Choose the color and type

96

of background suitable to the design and the article to be decorated.

2. Because of the slanting edge of a tray, the easiest way to copy the design onto a tray is to cut two or three small holes in the center of the tracing paper, which of course must not interfere with the design, and then place the original tracing in the proper position and fasten it to the tray through the holes. The loose edge makes it possible to fit the design *onto* the flange and make a more accurate tracing. Slip a piece of chalk paper, chalk side down, under the tracing and trace with a stylus.

3. Remove the tracing. Using the pattern as a guide, paint in exactly the same technique as that used on the pattern. Paint all the gold leaf and freehand bronzing first. This prevents any gold leaf or bronze powder from adhering to the painted design. Dry thoroughly. Protect the gold leaf and bronzing with a coat of varnish before proceeding with painting.

4. When all the decorating and striping is finished, proceed with the Final Varnish Finish as described on pp. 39–40.

5. Last but not least, mix varnish and gold powder in a small bottle cap. With a bowl point pen, sign on the back: "Hand decorated by (your name and date)."

ELEVENTH PROCESS

Lace-Edge Painting

Materials Needed

French quill square-tipped brushes. Art & Sign, series #475, various sizes (used for base coats of design only)

Sable water color brushes:

Art & Sign, Finepoint, series #9, sizes 00 and 1 through 8

Winsor Newton, Finest Sable, series #7, sizes 1 through 8

or M. Grumbacher, Finest Red Sable, series #197, sizes 1 through 8

or Art & Sign, Everpoint, series #8, sizes 1 through 8

Scrollers. Art & Sign, series #831 or #832, sizes 1 and 2

Tubes of artist oil colors:

Prussian blue	Striping white in japan
Alizarin crimson	Burnt umber
Chrome yellow medium	Raw umber
Yellow ochre	

Tube of Master Medium, Bohemian Guild Products

Small tube of English vermilion, Devoe #430

Frosted acetate

Black paper

Cardboard

Container for turpentine

Turpentine

Cleaning fluid

Tack cloth

Lard oil

98

Rags
Stylus
Bridge

    Bridge: How to make—Fasten bottle caps on each end of a ruler with masking tape.

Paint Mixtures for Lace-Edge Painting

Blue
- Prussian blue
- White
- English vermilion
- Sometimes a little yellow ochre

Green
- Yellow ochre
- Prussian blue
- English vermilion
- A little white

Grey
- English vermilion
- Prussian blue
- Striping white

Procedure

How to Make the Pattern

1. Make a tracing of the design in ink on tracing paper.

2. Make a paper pattern of the article to be decorated. Cut a piece of cardboard and cover it with black paper. Mark the boundaries of the paper pattern on the black paper with a white pencil. Mount the ink tracing on the black paper in the proper position. Cover it with piece of frosted acetate and fasten it at the corners only, with the frosted side up. This leaves enough room to slip a piece of black paper between the acetate and the tracing in order to test the semi-transparent colors while painting.

3. Lace-edge trays always have a very fine border, usually of gold leaf, close to the flange. The gold-leaf border must be completed and protected with a coat of varnish before painting the design.

4. Pour turpentine for cleaning the brushes into a container. Pour Nobles & Hoare quick-drying gold size into a bottle cap.

99

5. Mix English vermilion with gold size on the palette. Clean a quill brush and paint the basic color for the flowers, urns, or birds. Let dry twenty-four hours.

6. Mix Master medium wax and the colors to be used on the palette. Leave a quantity of wax unmixed on the palette.

7. Clean the oil out of several water color brushes with turpentine and wipe them dry. Select the proper water color brush and moisten it in the wax medium. Load the brush with the desired color and "puddle" the brush. Do not wipe out or "dress" the brush. Make a brush stroke with the loaded brush. The brush will leave ridges of paint which blend with the semi-transparent wax and show through the background color. Ridges of highlights fading into the background are a characteristic of this type of painting. Use a separate brush for each color and continue working in each color, one over the other, while the paint is still wet. Paints mixed with wax medium do not run into each other but stay in the position left by the brush stroke. This allows a great deal of freedom in painting. But do not work over the brush strokes as this will fuse the colors.

8. Green leaves are veined by working brush strokes of white into the wet green. Often yellow brush strokes are blended over the white. Fine vermilion lines are painted around the edges of rose leaves. Sometimes green leaves are painted over a red base coat which leaves a red glow around the edge. The entire lace-edge pattern can be completed at one time. Use a bridge in order to keep out of the wet paint.

9. Put the pattern aside in a dust-free place for a week or more. The wax medium takes a long time to dry.

10. When it is perfectly dry, protect it with a coat of varnish. Dry. Mount the pattern on black cardboard and cover it with clear acetate.

How to Apply the Design to the Article

1. Prepare a tortoise-shell background as described on p. 35–36 in "Backgrounds" or a flat black background if preferred.

2. Place the ink tracing of the original design in the proper position on the prepared article and fasten it with masking tape

100

through holes cut in between the various parts of the design. Copy the fine border close to the flange first by inserting chalk paper, chalk side down, and tracing with a stylus. Remove the tracing and lay on the gold-leaf border. Dry. Protect the border with several coats of varnish rubbed to a smooth dull finish.

3. Replace the tracing and trace on the remaining design using chalk paper and a stylus. Remove the tracing.

4. Mix the oil colors with the wax medium and proceed to paint the design in exactly the same technique as was used to paint on the pattern. Use the pattern as a guide from which to copy.

5. When all the painting is completed, allow plenty of time for the wax to dry. Varnish the surface and proceed with the Final Varnish Finish, as described on pp. 39–40.

6. Make a mixture of varnish and gold powder in a bottle cap. Use a bowl point pen and sign on the back: "Hand decorated by (your name and date)."

Bibliography

REFERENCES PERTAINING DIRECTLY TO THE TEXT

Striping:
Brazer, Esther Stevens: *Early American Decoration,* Pond-Ekberg Co., Springfield, Mass., pp. 62—65.

Tinting a Stenciled Pattern:
Brazer, Esther Stevens: *Early American Decoration,* Pond-Ekberg Co., Springfield, Mass., p. 51.

Freehand Brush Strokes:
Brazer, Esther Stevens: *Early American Decoration,* Pond-Ekberg Co., Springfield, Mass., pp. 57—61.

Gold Leaf:
Bond, Jessica H.: "How to Make Friends with Gold Leaf," *The Decorator,* Vol. III, No. 1, pp. 3—5.
Spellman, Joseph M.: "Gold Leaf and Pictorial Work on Glass," *The Decorator,* Vol. III, No. 2, pp. 7—12.

Floating Color:
Brazer, Esther Stevens: *Early American Decoration,* Pond-Ekberg Co., Springfield, Mass., pp. 89—92.
Burrows, Viola: "Floating Color," *The Decorator,* Vol. III, No. 2, p. 35.

Lace-Edge Painting:
Burrows, Viola: "Lace-Edge Trays," *The Decorator,* Vol. V, No. 2, pp. 15—16.
Clark, Mary Jane: "Painting a Lace-Edge Tray," *The Decorator,* Vol. VI, No. 2, pp. 23—24.

REFERENCE BOOKS

The following books and the list of articles from *The Decorator* in the third section of this bibliography provide the student with a list of readings through which he may become more familiar with the historical background of early American decoration and techniques to supplement the basic ones described in this book. Continuous research is being carried on in this field, and the list of articles points out some of the most important findings.

Art and Science of Gilding, The, Hastings and Co., New York, N.Y. (out-of-print, but may be borrowed from the publisher, 150 Fifth Avenue, for a $10 deposit.)

Bartlett, Morton: *The Bench and Brush Manual of Groundwork and Finishing,* Bench and Brush Publishers, (no longer in existence).

———: *Decorative Painting, Stenciling, and Gilding,* Country Loft, Newfields, N.H.

Brazer, Esther Stevens: *Early American Decoration,* Pond-Ekberg Co., Springfield, Mass.

Christensen, Edwin O.: *Index of American Design,* Macmillan Co., New York, N.Y.

Cramer, Edith: *Early American Decoration,* Charles T. Bransford Co., Boston, Mass.

Devoe, Shirley Spaulding: *How to Paint Tin,* Privately printed, Bridgewater, Conn. (out-of-print).

Dickinson, George: *English Papier-Mâché,* Courier Press, London, (out-of-print).

Guilders' Tips, Hastings and Co., New York, N.Y.

Gilding on Glass, Wood, or Metal, George E. Watson Co., Chicago, Ill.

Gould, Mary Earle: *Antique Tin and Tole Ware: Its History and Romance,* Charles E. Tuttle Co., Rutland, Vt.

Grotz, George: *Gunk to Glow: The Furniture Doctor,* Town Clerk's Corner, Killingworth, Conn.

Hallett, Charles: *Furniture Decoration Made Easy,* Charles T. Bransford Co., Boston, Mass.

Hoke, Elizabeth S.: *Painted Tray and Freehand Bronzing,* Mrs. C. Noonan Keyser, Plymouth Meeting, Pa.

———: *Pennsylvania-German Painted Tin,* Mrs. C. Noonan Keyser, Plymouth Meeting, Pa.

Holloway, Edward S.: *The Practical Book of American Furniture and Decoration,* Halcyon House, New York, N.Y.

John, W. D.: *English Decorated Trays,* The Ceramic Book Co., Newport Mon., England.

———: *Pontypool and Usk Japanned Ware,* The Ceramic Book Co., Newport Mon., England.

104

Lea, Zilla Rider, ed.: *The Ornamented Chair: Its Development in America,* Charles E. Tuttle Co., Rutland, Vt.

Lichten, Frances: *Folk Art of Rural Pennsylvania,* Charles Scribner's Sons, New York, N.Y.

Lipman, Jean: *American Folk Decoration,* Oxford University Press, New York, N.Y.

Murray, Maria: *The Art of Tray Painting,* The Studio Publications, Inc., New York, N.Y. (out-of-print).

Nutting, Wallace: *Furniture Treasury,* Old America Co., Framingham, Mass.

Powers, Beatrice Farnsworth, and Olive Floyd: *Early American Decorated Tinware,* E. P. Lynch, Providence, R.I.

Sabine, Ellen S.: *American Antique Decoration,* D. Van Nostrand Co., Inc., Princeton, N.J.

————: *American Folk Art,* D. Van Nostand Co., Inc., Princeton, N.J.

————: *Early American Decorative Patterns,* D. Van Nostrand Co., Inc., Princeton, N.J.

Toller, Jane: *Papier-Mâché in Great Britain and America,* G. Bell and Sons, Ltd., London, England.

Waring, Janet: *Early American Stencils on Walls and Furniture,* William R. Scott, New York, N.Y.

Wright, Florence: *How to Stencil a Chair,* The Workshop, Pen Yan, N.Y.

Yates, Raymond F.: *Hobby Book of Stenciling and Brush Stroke Painting,* McGraw-Hill and Co., New York, N.Y.

Zoller, Jane: *Papier-Mache in England and America,* The Ceramic Book Co., Newport Mon., England.

ARTICLES FROM *THE DECORATOR*

The Decorator is a periodical published semi-annually by the Esther Stevens Brazer Guild of the Historical Society of American Decoration, Inc., in which appear new reports on recent research. *The Decorator* may be obtained by writing to Miss Jean Wylie, Post Road, Darien Review Building, Box 894, Darien, Connecticut.

Baker, Muriel L.: "The Pattisons of Berlin," Vol. VIII, No. 2 (1954), p. 8.

Devoe, Shirley: "Notes on Hitchcock Chairs," Vol. VI, No. 1 (1951), p. 17.

Holmes, Evelyn: "Painted Tip Top Tables," Vol. V, No. 1 (1951), p. 8.

Kriebel, Rev. Lester K.: "A Brief History of Pennsylvania German Illuminated Writings," Vol. VI, No. 2 (1952), p. 17.

Muller, Mrs. Max: "Esther Stevens Brazer Collection of Early American Designs," Vol. IV, No. 1 (1949), p. 16.

Murray, Maria: "Oriental Lacquer Work," Vol. VI, No. 1 (1952), p. 5.

Robacker, Earl F.: "Painted Tinware of Pennsylvania," Vol. III, No. 2 (1949), p. 13.

Robinson, Everett N.: "Country Tin of Oliver Filley," Vol. II, No. 2 (1948), p. 15.

————: "Is It Typical Connecticut or Pennsylvania Dutch?," Vol. III, No. 2 (1949), p. 19.

Scott, Violet M.: "A Guide for Beginners to Early American Decoration," Vol. I, No. 1 (1946), p. 14.

————: "My Story, Esther Stevens Brazer," Vol. V, No. 2 (1951), p. 7.

Stone, Dorothy D.: "History of Bellows," Vol. VII, No. 2 (1953), p. 5.

"The Tin Peddler," Vol. V, No. 2 (1951), p. 17.

Wilson, Nadine: "Authentic Oriental Lacquer Ware," Vol. XIV, No. 1 (1959), p. 8.

Wright, Florence: "Some Decorated Chairs of the 1800's, "Vol. I, No. 2 (1947), p. 4.

Wright, Walter Herron: "The Butlers of Brandy Hill," Vol. VII, No. 1 (1953), p. 9.

Addresses for Materials

Abrasive Products, Inc., South Braintree 85, Massachusetts. Jewelite waterproof paper.

Alexander's Paint Store, 137–02 Northern Boulevard, Flushing, New York. Giles black seal varnish.

A. Meilinger and Sons, 158 East Avenue, Hicksville, New York. Stencil scissors; experts in sharpening fine scissors.

American Rattan and Reed Manufacturing Co., 268 Norman Avenue, Brooklyn 22, New York. Chair cane.

Art and Sign Brush Manufacturing Co., 36–32 34th Street, Long Island City, New York. Art and Sign scrollers and brushes.

Arthur Brown and Brothers, Inc., 2 West 46th Street, New York, New York. Artists' materials.

Bainbridge, Kimpton, and Haupt, Inc., 218 Greenwich Street, New York 8, New York. National steel rulers.

Behr-Manning Co. (division of Norton Co.), Troy, New York. Hard Arkansas oilstone.

B. Polivy and Sons, Inc., 1644 Second Avenue, New York 28, New York. Pratt and Lambert products.

Chair-Loc Co., Lakehurst, New Jersey. Chair-Loc.

Charles Bruning Co., Inc., 125 North Street, Teterboro, New Jersey. Guil-Trace tracing cloth.

Chester P. Galleher, 105 Puritan Road, Rosslyn Farms, Carnegie, Pennsylvania. Crystallized cut-corner or coffin trays.

Country Loft, Main Street, Newfields, New Hampshire. Tinware, lace-edge trays, and materials for decorating.

Craftint Manufacturing Co., 450 Seventh Avenue, New York, New York. Sign craft colors.

Crafts Manufacturing Co., Massachusetts Avenue, Luenburg, Massachusetts. Tinware, primed and blacked; Devoe English vermilion; and supplies.

107

C. Schrack and Co., 150–158 North 4th Street, Philadelphia 6, Pennsylvania. Paints and varnishes.

C. S. Osborne & Co.. Inc., 125 Jersey Street, Harrison, New Jersey. Revolving leather punch #225, dental supplies secondhand, and rubber dam punch.

Early American Chair Co., 110$\frac{1}{2}$ Cross Street, Lawrence, Massachusetts. Early American chairs, authentic Boston rockers, and Hitchcock chairs.

Edroy Products Co., Grand Central Palace Building, 480 Lexington Avenue, New York, New York. All-purpose magnifying glasses.

Empire Artists' Materials, 851 Lexington Avenue, New York, New York. Bronze lining powders, brushes, and oil paints.

E. P. Lynch, Inc., 92 Weybossett Street, Providence, Rhode Island. Tinware and materials for decorating.

Franklin and Lennon Paint Co., Inc., 537 West 125th Street, New York 27, New York. McClosley Heirloom crystal clear varnish and other paints.

George E. Watson Co., 417 South Wabash Avenue, Chicago 5, Illinois. Gold-leaf supplies and artists' materials.

Griffin Manufacturing Co., 1656 Ridge Road East, Webster, New York. Grifhold tools.

Hastings and Co., 43 West 16th Street, New York, New York. Gold leaf.

Hatfield's, 859 Boylston Steet, Boston 16, Massachusetts. Bohemian Wax, Master Medium.

Hazen Paper Co., Holyoke, Massachusetts. Hazencote black paper.

H. Behlen and Brothers, Inc., 10 Christopher Street, New York 14, New York. Nobles and Hoare quick-drying gold size.

Henry Lindenmeyer and Sons, 53rd Avenue at 11th Street, Long Island City, New York. Dura-Glo black paper.

Joseph Mayer Co., Inc., 5 Union Square, New York, New York. Artists' materials.

King and Walters, 27 Ferry Street, New York 38, New York. Chair-seating materials.

Koh-i-Noor Pencil Co., Inc., Bloomsbury, New Jersey. Koh-i-Noor Rapidograph pen #00.

L. Hitchcock Chair Co., Riverton, Connecticut. Decorated furniture only.

Lowe Brothers Co., Eastern District, 335 Grand Street, Jersey City 2, New Jersey. Yellow plax and flat black enameloid.

Major Services, M. A. Jacobson, 1740 West Columbia Avenue, Chicago 26, Illinois. Frosted Protectoid Craft-X #3 and crystal clear (send for circular).

Master Bronze Co., Calumet City, Illinois. De Rusto-P.C.-77 clear (primer coat for metal).

Merit-Vin-Sons, Inc., 227 East 44th Street, New York 17, New York. Wilson Imperial products.

Milton Paper Co., Inc., 100 West 22nd Street, New York, New York. Black Croyden.

M. Swift and Sons, 10 Love Lane, Hartford, Connecticut. Deep gold leaf.

Novis Paint Co., Inc., 899 Post Road, Darien, Connecticut. Milwaukee ink and Baer Brothers bronze powders.

Old Guilford Forge on the Green, Winthrop Humphrey and James Miller, Proprietors, Guilford, Connecticut. Tinware.

Park Studios, P. O. Box 28P, Arlington Heights 75, Massachusetts. Tinware and everything for the decorator.

Pearl Paint Co., 105 Chambers Street, New York, New York. Murphy's black asphaltum

Plaza Paint Supply Corp., 1026 Third Avenue, New York, New York. Paints.

Pratt and Lambert, Inc., 33–01 38th Avenue, Long Island City, New York. #61 floor varnish, clear.

Rusticide Products Co., 3125 Perkins Avenue, Cleveland 14, Ohio. Rust-i-cide.

S. D. Jacobs Co., Inc., 455 West 28th Street, New York, New York. DuPont products and lacquers.

Stone Co., Inc., 12 North Street, Danbury, Connecticut. Decorating supplies and tinware.

Thomson's Art Store, 171 Grand, White Plains, New York. Artists' materials.

Tinker Shop, 142 West Main Street, Milford, Connecticut. Tinware and materials for decorating.

Valentine and Co., Inc., 11 East 36th Street, New York 16, New York. Valspar.

Village Tin Shop. W. H. Doble, Jr., Proprietor, 1030 Main Street, Hingham, Massachusetts. Tinware and materials for decorating.

Wilson Imperial Co., 115 Chestnut Street, Newark 5, New Jersey. Imperial Rapid brush cleaner and Imperial Wonder Paste paint remover.

109

Index

Allgood, Edward, 17
Allgood, Thomas, 17
application of the stencil, process, 50–58; materials needed, 50; procedure, 52–58

background, materials needed, 31–32
background, painting the:
  antiqued, 37–38
  artificial graining on wood, 36–37
  bronze (dusted), 36
  dusted; *see* bronze
  solid opaque, 35
  tortoise-shell, 35–36
  transparent with asphaltum varnish, 35
background, preparation of:
  new tin, 34
  new wood, 34
  old tin, how to strip, 33–34
  old wood, how to strip, 34
  original design, how to preserve, 32–33
  primer coat for tin, 34
background, varnishing the (varnish):
  final varnish finish, 39–40
  preliminary varnish, 38–39
bobs, preparation of, 52
Brazer, Esther Stevens, 15

Brazer Guild, 16
brush strokes, freehand, 67–77
brushes, care of, 64–65
brushes, quill, inserting handles, 64
burnt varnish ball, how to make, 40–41

chalk paper, how to make, 78–79
composite stencils, 42
country painting, process, 78–81; materials needed, 78; procedure, 79–81
cutting the stencil, process, 46–49; materials needed, 46; procedure, 46; suggestions, 46–49

early American decoration, 15–16

floating color, process, 93–97; materials needed, 93–94; procedure, 94–97
freehand bronze, process, 82–85; materials needed, 82; procedure, 82–85
freehand brush strokes, process, 67–77; materials needed, 67–68; procedure, 69–77

gold leaf, process, 86–92; materials needed, 86–87; procedure, 87–92;

japanning, 17

lace-edge painting, process, 98–101;
materials needed, 98–99; procedure,
99–101
leaves (veining), 54–56, 100

materials, complete list: bronze powders, 27
brushes, 23–26
miscellaneous, 28–30
paints and varnishes, 27–28
tools, 22–23
varnishes, 28

one-piece stencils, 42

paint mixtures, lace-edge painting, 99
paint mixtures, opaque, 68–69
paint mixtures, transparent, 68
palette, velour, preparation of, 50–52
Patterson, Edward and William (Pattison), 21
Pattison; see Patterson
practice pad, how to make, 59

scroller, 70
striping, process, 59–62; materials
needed, 59; procedure, 59–62; suggestions, 62

tack cloth, how to make, 40

tin plate, 17, 21
tinting the stencil, process, 63–66;
materials needed, 63–64; procedure,
65–66
tracing a stencil pattern, process, 42–45;
materials needed, 42; procedure
43–44; suggestions, 45
trays, types of:
Chippendale (Gothick, pie crust),
19–20
coffin; see country tin
country tin (octagonal, coffin), 21
deep-edged octagonal, 19
gallery, 19
Gothic Sandwich, 19–20
lace-edge (Revere), 17–19
oblong stenciled, 20–21
octagonal; see country tin
Queen Anne, 21
rectangular, 19
Revere; see lace-edge

varnish; see background, varnishing the
varnish, dull, 43
veiling, 96
veining; see leaves
velvet finger, preparation of, 52

work table, 65